A HISTORY OF
BRAY

A HISTORY OF
BRAY

Arthur Flynn

TEMPUS

Dedicated to Damian

First published 2004

Tempus Publishing Limited
The Mill, Brimscombe Port,
Stroud, Gloucestershire, GL5 2QG
www.tempus-publishing.com

© Arthur Flynn, 2004

British Library Cataloguing in Publication Data.
A catalogue record for this book is available from the British Library.

ISBN 0 7524 3269 9

Typesetting and origination by Tempus Publishing Limited
Printed in Great Britain

CONTENTS

FOREWORD

I am delighted to be invited to write a brief introduction to a book on the history of Bray, where I grew up from the age of two to eleven. These are undoubtedly the formative years in anyone's life, and also the ones which one remembers with the greatest vividness.

Of course, Bray was a much smaller place then than it is now, and much of the area around the town which is now built up was still open country. I was fortunate in that my mother was determined that I should take a lot of exercise, and so from the age of five to nine she sent me out for walks in the afternoon with a wonderful companion, a Miss Cuddy, then in her mid-fifties. She survived to become a centenarian with all her faculties intact, and followed with great interest the performances of the first coalition government in which I was a minister.

Miss Cuddy had no belief in walking along roads when there were fields or gardens on either side that one could explore. As a result of her cheerful disregard for private property I got to know intimately the area from the Great Sugar Loaf south to Shankill and inland to Enniskerry and the Scalp.

Occasionally life was punctuated by major events – such as the fire in the garage at the bottom of the Main Street, when, if my recollection is correct, the fire engine would not start and had to be pushed down the Main Street – and, a year later, the explosion of a tar machine, on Killarney Road, a couple of hundred yards from our house. Major events like that stand out in a child's memory.

In summer much of my time was spent at the beach. Even to reach the beach Miss Cuddy felt that the best way was to go through the grounds of Loreto Convent rather than to follow the public road. My memory of making sand-castles on the beach includes an early concern for environmental problems – I always provided them with pipes down to the sea to carry the sewerage, made of sticks.

On Bray Head there was an amusement centre which had a feature which I have not come across since then – bumping boats as distinct from bumping cars, a gentler sport and one that I think could usefully be revived.

There were also the pierrot shows and the Punch and Judy show on the esplanade. My parents were temporarily well off as the result of a legacy (for the only time in their lives). We lived in a large house with three acres of garden and thirteen acres of farmland around it which were let to a nearby farmer. His cows provided excellent targets for bow and arrow practice – it's hard to miss a stationary cow. For a period we had a cow of our own who provided fresh milk and rich cream, but unfortunately she got ill and died. We then had to revert to the milkman who came to the side window near the kitchen each day with his huge metal can of milk and the metal container to dole it out.

My parents were extremely sociable people, and most weekends – or so it seems in retrospect – the house was full of people coming to play tennis, or to go for walks in the surrounding countryside, the evening being rounded off with charades in the drawing room.

Occasionally there were distinguished visitors – shadowy figures now in my memory, such as W.B. Yeats, T.S. Eliot and Jacques Maritain. My memories are much clearer of such close family friends such as Ernest and Annie Blythe; Paddy and Annie McGilligan; Sean and Margaret McEntee; Dr Dick Hayes; Edward and Christine Longford; and many friends of my elder brothers. Also of course my Northern grandmother, and uncles and aunts from the United States, Canada and Britain, as well as many cousins, mainly from the North.

It couldn't last; it didn't. In March 1937 the house had to be sold in a vain attempt to bring expenditure within the limits of income. But they were wonderful years, full of happy memories and Bray as a result always has a very special place in my life.

My only regret is that the place where we lived, Fairy Hill, has now been built over with such uninhibited enthusiasm that not a stone lies upon a stone, not a tree remains, to remind me of our home of those days in the late 1920s and 1930s.

Garret Fitzgerald

PREFACE AND ACKNOWLEDGEMENTS

Over the past decade I have had many requests to have my *History of Bray* republished or to write a new updated edition. Finally I have combined both requests. Many things and people had prompted me to write this long-overdue history of Bray. Previous historical records of the town's heritage and culture are contained in the outdated *A Hundred Years of Bray* by an 'Old Inhabitant', *The Stones of Bray* by Reverend George Digby Scott first published in 1913, passing references in *The Neighbourhood of Dublin* by Weston St John Joyce and Colbert Martin's two fine books *A Drink from Broderick's Well* and *A Bridge Below the Town*. There were also journals from the Cualann Historical Society and the Old Bray Society. On reading two comprehensive local histories – *Listowel* by Fr J.A. Gaughan and *Dun Laoghaire* by Peter Pearson – I saw the potential for a book on Bray.

Many facets of Bray's past were of interest to me and for many years I have been accumulating a collection of newspaper cuttings, references and snippets of local history. I undertook extensive research on Bray in the Public Records Office, the National Library and various local sources with the intention of uncovering hitherto unpublished facts. Lord Meath generously made the family diaries available to me. Bray has had a strong literary tradition, with James Joyce, Oscar Wilde, Sir Walter Scott and Sheridan Le Fanu among the writers who resided for periods in the town. John Millington Synge and Roger Casement were pupils at Aravon School. In a political context the town has had an impressive past. Cearbhall O'Dalaigh, who later became President, was born at 85 Main Street. Desmond FitzGerald spent a long period of his life in the town and his son Garret lived and attended school there. Bray was a film-making centre as far back as 1918 when the silent-screen director Billy Power produced several feature films.

In attending lectures by Michael Ledwidge on 'The Development of Bray', by Ross Connolly on 'Trade Unionism in Bray', by John O'Donovan on 'Bray Characters' and by Peter Aspell on 'The History of the Brabazon Family' I discovered new and unexplored areas of the town's history.

Finally, I relished the challenge of tracing Bray's changing face from being a small Viking settlement, through the Norman invasion, the advent of the railway and its subsequent new prosperity which earned it the title of 'the Brighton of Ireland', to the present sprawling commuter town of 27,000-plus.

I would like to thank the following for their assistance in my preparation of this book: Michael Kelleher and Tom French of Bray Library, Patrick Melvin of the Dáil Library, Mary Davies of the Royal Irish Academy, Lord Meath, Jim Brophy, Robert Butler and Noelle Ringwood of Ballywaltrim Library, Paddy Murphy, Michael Hartnett, Diarmuid Breathnach, Henry Cairns, Fr J.A. Gaughan, Public Record Office, John Byrne, Brian White, Kathleen Kinsella, Michael Lawlor, Blaise Tracey, Gilbert Library, Eileen Murray, Damian Flynn and Dick Roche.

1

THE BEGINNING

The town of Bray, lying 12 miles south of Dublin and 19 miles north of Wicklow, on either side of the Dargle River (*dair-glan*, glen of oaks) and nestling in the shadow of Bray Head and the Sugarloaf Mountains, has undergone many name changes through the centuries. It is strongly believed that the name Bray evolved from the clan name of Ui Briuin Cualann who, in the course of time, changed their name to Brien. Old church records, however, refer to the town as 'Bre', indicating that it may derive its name from the Gaelic word *bri* (hill or rising ground) – a reference to Bray Head and the many steep inclines surrounding the town. When the Norman Sir Walter de Ridelsford built a castle in 1174, he named it the castle of Bre and the area surrounding it the Barony of Bre. De Ridelsford also took possession of a church that he called Derdac. We find mention of 'the colleges of Derdac', which may have existed before De Ridelsford's time. 'Derichat' and 'Derdach' are probably all forms of the Irish *dear-teach* or *deathach*, which mean 'a house of penitence' or 'oratory'.

Maurice O'Regan, secretary and interpreter to Dermot MacMurrough, King of Leinster, when writing the history of Strongbow's invasion in 1177 said 'Maurice Fitzgerald got the county of O'Felin, formerly the estate of MacKelan, lying between Bree and Arklow.'

Sir James Ware in his *Antiquities of Ireland*, published in 1639, wrote: 'Bray Head is a high and large cape, stretching a considerable way into the sea on the south side of the Bay of Dublin, from which a river and town take their names.' Perhaps it was so called because of the resemblance it bears to a neck, for which the Irish is *braighe*, or from *bri*, a hill.

In the fourteenth century the area south of the river was called Muche Bree and later Greate Bray and Old Bray; the northern side was Lythe Bree. A Venetian map of about 1570 shows an undefined 'Brey M' between Dublin and Wicklow. When Sir William Petty undertook the Down Survey in 1654, both the village and its anglicised name were well established. Until recently the official Irish name for the town was Bri Cualann but it has now reverted to the original Bre.

The course of the river, referred to as Brey Flumen, is well defined in John Speed's map of Leinster (1610). A village called Old Court close to its mouth presumably refers to the castle, built nearly a mile south of the river in 1440. The earliest documents to mention the river refer to 'The Water of Brien' because it drained the heart of the district occupied by the tribe. For a considerable period it was called Bray River but eventually became known as the Dargle River. The origin of the name 'Dargle' has been a constant source of debate. Many suggest that it comes from the Celtic *dair glin*, translating as 'Dark Glen' or 'Glen of Oaks', but Weston St John Joyce maintained that it came from the Irish *dearg*, meaning 'red', and that *deargail*, now Dargle, means 'a little red spot'. Rising near the Sally Gap in the Wicklow Mountains at a point 1,770ft in altitude, the river skirts War Hill, where a tributary cascades down the mountainside to form the magnificent Powerscourt waterfall. Then it passes the celebrated oak-wooded gorge and protruding Lover's Leap; of its many tributaries the largest is the Glencree River that rises at Lough Bray and the smallest, a modern stream, runs from Killruddery estate.

The many ancient church sites which surround the town bear witness to its historic past but even older are the prehistoric features of Bray Head, with its area of Cambrian rocks laid down during the Palaeolithic era between 200 and 500 million years ago. There are three areas of Cambrian rocks in Ireland, all located on the east coast. The series that stretches from Bray to Wicklow is well exposed at Bray and Greystones. The south side of Bray Head is a prime example, where green and purple colours show alternating layers of different textures interwoven with greywacke sandstone and quartzite (sandstone which has been subject to intense heat and pressure). These strata are clearly visible in many railway cuttings where they can be seen in layers of some 4 to 6ft. Fossils related to the sea urchin (*Eldonia antonii*) were found in a cave called the Brandy Hole. Fan-like impressions, termed *Oldhamia radiata*, were discovered at Bray in 1844 and are classed as marine algae. However, there is a theory that these were merely frost stencilling in mud later hardened by the elements. The Bray series of Cambrian rocks are amongst the oldest formations in the world.

More evidence of the town's ancient past lies in the submerged primeval forest at the north beach, the remains of which can be partially seen at low spring tides. It has a radiocarbon age of 6,750 years. Originally a dense forest covered much of the coast east of the town but through coastal erosion and the gradual development of the town it receded.

There is no evidence that the Romans ever actually invaded Ireland but there is substantial proof indicating that the Romans did arrive in Bray. We know this because of a find by workmen digging foundations on the beach near the base of Bray Head in 1835. A description of their discovery is as follows:

> The workmen were surprised to meet with the skeletons of several human bodies which, on further examination, they found to be placed not confusedly heaped together as the slain of battle, but in graves placed regularly side by side. Each was separated from its neighbour by a partition of flags or stone. On exposure to the air the bones crumbled; the teeth alone were more durable and in tolerable preservation. The most remarkable circumstances connected with these skeletons were a number of Roman copper coins, one or two of which lay on or beside the breast of each. Of these coins, which were about the size of a penny piece, some bore the image and inscription of Adrian and the others those of Trajan in clear and distinct outline.

As the Romans never formed any settlements in Ireland the question naturally arises as to how the skeletons and coins were buried in this location. The answer would appear to be that they were probably those of the crew of some Roman galley which had been wrecked on the shore off Bray, with some of the survivors performing the funeral rituals. The coins, it is presumed, were the fee designated for the grim Ferryman and part of the funeral rite that could not be neglected.

Shortly after their arrival the Vikings (or Ostmen as they were also called) established many bases from which to plunder the countryside. They soon learned that the richest monasteries were all inland but the rivers were like highways to the Viking longships, which, with their shallow draught, could penetrate far upstream. They secured a river by establishing a base at its mouth that they defended with a wall and rough fortifications. Bray was an obvious choice for landing and the area was handed over to the Turchil family whose domain extended from Donnybrook to Glencree.

Glendalough was burned and plundered by the Vikings for the first time in 830 and some subsequent raids were carried out from Bray. In Viking times the land lying between Bray and Dublin was called *Dubh-gall*, or Lands of the Black Foreigners, who were the Danes, to differentiate it from *Fin-gall*, which lay on the north side of Dublin and was inhabited by the Norwegians, or White Foreigners.

In Bray at the time of the Vikings' arrival there was little more than a small oratory or *deas-teach*, a primitive edifice where St Paul's Church stands today, and a few small dwellings.

2

THE COMING OF
THE NORMANS

He gave him also Wicklow
Between Bree and Arklow
This was the land of Kilmantain
Between Ath Cliath and Loch Garman.

This extract is from *The Song of Dermot and the Earls* by an unknown Norman author, written around 1225. Although the song mentions Bree it is unlikely that there was any substantial settlement there before the Anglo-Norman invasion. The territory was known as Uí Briuin Cualann at the time of the invasion in 1169 and was shared by Dermot MacMurrough's son-in-law Domhnall MacGilla-Mo-Choluic (a form of this name remains in Cattigollagher, the rocky summit north of Ballyman) and the son of the Dublin Viking chief Turchil. King Henry II of England fully appreciated the importance of the ports and seashore on the east coast and the entire littoral from Bray to Wicklow and for some distance inland was taken over and occupied by Norman adventurers.

The Anglo-Norman invasion began as a result of a dispute between the king of Leinster, Dermot MacMurrough, and Tiarnan Ó Ruairc of Breifne. In 1152 the feud worsened when MacMurrough kidnapped Ó Ruairc's wife and held her hostage. In time Ó Ruairc and MacMurrough's enemies joined forces and attacked his base in Ferns and banished him. MacMurrough set out for Wales to muster support to retain his territory. Richard fitz Gilbert de Clare, better known as Strongbow, agreed to assist him but on a number of terms. Strongbow wanted to be king of Leinster following the death of MacMurrough and also to marry MacMurrough's eldest daughter, Aoife. MacMurrough agreed to the conditions, thereby opening the way for the first Anglo-Norman invasion.

Following the invasion, the Norman knight and adventurer Sir Walter de Ridelsford distinguished himself by combating the Vikings' unsuccessful counter-attack on Dublin in 1171 when Askulv Mac Turchil, the former Danish governor of Dublin, was killed. De Ridelsford was credited with killing the Viking John the Mad or John the Wood in the battle and with saving the life of Sir Milo de Cogan. Richard de Clare, Earl of Pembroke, then Lord Deputy, granted the manor of the Lordship of Bre to de Ridelsford in 1173. He also received several 'carucates' of land, covering approximately the area from the poundhouse (the present Town Hall) to Sunnybank and from the sea to Crow Bank (opposite the end of the People's Park). The small oratory was to develop into the parochial church of Bre, the principal church of the deanery of Bre that extended from Monkstown and Stillorgan in the north to Newcastle in the south. Milo de Cogan's son, Richard later married Basilia, a daughter of de Ridelsford, and land in Ballymakelly was granted to him on the occasion of the marriage.

In 1174 de Ridelsford built the great feudal castle of Bre, which was constructed of wood, surrounded by a strong wall on the high ground to the south of Bre Water near the present bridge. The castle was in a prime defensive position, situated on the cliff overhanging the river and was impregnable against attack from either direction. As the castle required servants and tradesmen, several cottages were built and a village grew up around it on both sides of the river. The charter conveying the lands to de Ridelsford was most unsatisfactory and he had it renewed in 1185 by Prince John who definitely outlined names and places granted to him and roughly stated their acreage. Not only did the Normans take over the town; they also extended its boundary and established it as a defence settlement, as it was on the edge of the Norman-dominated Pale. It became one of the chief fortresses for southern County Dublin.

When Bre was granted to de Ridelsford, a boundary ran through the centre of the parish. Killruddery and Rathdown remained in the possession of Domhnall Mac Giollomacholmog, along with the townlands of Giltspur and Deerpark. By a deed of 1196–99 Domhnall's son Dermot granted one carucate of land in Killruddery to Richard de Felda in return for a pair of gilt spurs to be presented to him and his heirs each year at Michaelmas. Later Dermot granted his entire holding at Killruddery to de Felda with the exception of a small portion held by a Hamo Rufus, for an annual payment of two gold pieces. For about a century after the arrival of de Ridelsford, Bre enjoyed peace and prosperity and was little affected by the skirmishes devastating other parts of the country. De Ridelsford left no male heir and on his death his estates were divided between his two daughters.

In 1225 St Mary's Abbey (situated in what is now Mary Street, Dublin) was granted a burgage in Bre which consisted of 2 acres of arable land, gave full rights to burghers and granted licences to bring boats up the river to trade with the Abbey of St Thomas. Soon afterwards de Cogan granted to St Thomas' Abbey a tenure in Bre close to the burghage assigned to the monks of St Mary's at a yearly rent of 30 marks with a fine of 60 marks. Records from a lawsuit in 1223 show that the total extent of Killruddery was then approximately two carucates of land. The Abbey retained possession throughout the thirteenth century, paying the rent to Dermot's descendants until they redeemed it in 1280. In 1248 the king, on learning that the lands held by de Ridelsford at his death were occupied by others while the king still held custody of them, ordered that they should be restored to Stephen Longespee and his wife Emeline and to Elulo of Geneva and his wife Christina, the heirs of de Ridelsford.

The lands of Corke, which extended along the sea shore from Little Bray to Shanganagh, then called Kiltuck, were owned in the year 1200 by the Crown and were held under it by Fulk de Cantilupe. Some years later there were unsuccessful negotiations for their purchase from him on behalf of the chief governor of Ireland, Meyler FitzHenry, a natural son of Henry II. Later the crown resumed possession of the lands and they were leased for a time to the Priory of the Holy Trinity, then owners of the adjoining lands of Kiltuck. Towards the close of the thirteenth century, the land was granted to Geoffrey de Lyseham, a subject of the king of France. On the western side of Little Bray, beyond the lands of Old Connaught that were part of de Ridelsford's manor, lay the lands of Glenmudder or Ballyman, in a wooded glen. In the thirteenth century they were held by the Knights Templar, who had a house in Clontarf.

Bray was now a corporate town and amongst its rulers in the thirteenth century was Robert Chapman, bailiff of the town, and Philip Makagan, dean of the town. The residents included a lawless fishing community, for whose misdeeds the town sometimes suffered. On one occasion a fine was levied on the inhabitants owing to bodies having been buried without an inquest and wreckage having been concealed. A weekly market was granted to the town, as well as a licence to catch hares and foxes in the king's forests in Ireland.

One Irish family adopted the name Bray as a surname. At the end of the thirteenth century one of its members, Robert de Bray, who supplied the viceroy with skins and sent wine to Wales for the use of the English army, was appointed Lord Mayor of Dublin.

The manor of Bre was included in the possession assigned to the Crown by de Ridelsford's descendant Christiana de Marisco. In 1290 the manor was granted to Sir Theobald Butler, an ancestor of the house of Ormond, for the services of an armed horseman to be sent when required, fully equipped, to the gates of Dublin Castle. Amongst the principal tenants in the manor of Bre in 1284 were the Knights Templar, Robert the Baker who ran a successful mill adjoining the castle, and the Vicar of Bray.

On 16 April 1310 the native rebels launched a successful attack and destroyed the Castle of Bre. Edward de Botcher routed the attackers and in the ensuing battle 500 were slain. Soon afterwards the castle was rebuilt in granite and traces of its base are still visible in Church Lane.

At the time of the Bruce invasion in 1313, Bray, Arklow and Newcastle had been attacked and burned by the O'Tooles and the O'Byrnes. Thereafter the lands around Bray lay waste for many years. Sir Hugh de Lawless, a member of a family that became all-powerful in the district, was appointed by the crown in 1314 as Constable of Bray Manor. He resigned his commission five years later, stating that the lands, which on the arrival of the Scottish enemies of the king had been invaded, burned and totally devastated by the Irish, were still unprofitable and uncultivated. His only personal gain from the custody of the manor had been a gift of two salmon, but when he was charged rents they were returned to him by the author-ities as compensation for his effort to uphold English rule.

In order to protect the loyalist inhabitants of the district, a number of military stations were maintained between Bray and the Pale. In Bray a fortress was constructed from the ruins of de Ridelsford's castle which had escaped the general destruction. In 1334 Geoffrey Crump was given a lease of the manor at a rent of £6 1s 8½d per annum. The property was free from rent for the first two years on condition that he completed the reconstruc-tion. A militia force was raised from the garrison at Bray by a levy on the landowners between Bray and Dublin, including the priory of the Holy Trinity in respect of Kill-of-the-Grange and the Abbey of Saint Mary the Virgin in respect of Monkstown. Heavy and light horsemen and archers were supplied but at times the militia proved inefficient and in 1355 the garrison at Bray, unable to suppress the enemy, were replaced by chosen mounted men-at-arms, twenty light horsemen and forty archers under the command of Sir John de Bermingham.

For over three centuries the Wicklow Mountains remained the impen-etrable stronghold of the O'Tooles and the O'Brynes, who launched many successful raids on Bray. The Normans had dispossessed these tribes of their rich lands in Kildare and the embittered families had taken refuge in County Wicklow. In these hit and run raids they destroyed property and stole livestock before retreating into the dense woodlands where it was impossible for their Norman pursuers to detect them. The English within the Pale had to be prepared for their frequent and unexpected raids and a regular garrison of 1,100 men was maintained in Bre to defend the town. A Viceroy is reported as saying 'Your Majesty's laws are not obeyed within sight of the smoke of Dublin'. Eventually O'Toole, the local Wicklow chief, was paid £740 a year in 'black rent', or protection money, by the authori-ties to ensure they would not be attacked. Mac Murchadha received black rent for protecting the roads through Leinster.

Richard of Shrewsbury, Duke of Norfolk and Lieutenant of Ireland, granted custody of all the castles, manors and lordships of Bre and Killruddery to Walter, the Abbot of the House of the Blessed Virgin Mary near Dublin, at the rent of one shilling. Frequent changes of landowner resulted in a series of land grievances that caused unrest for over two centuries. Maurice Howell, in the early part of the century, had accounted to the Crown for the Bray rents. In 1316 a man named Harold was indicted for stealing timber from the Prior of Glenmudder. At the end of the century the Archbold and Lawless families were the main inhabitants. The Archbolds, who were regarded as protectors of the Pale, appear in the four-teenth century as tenants on the southern side of the river. Maurice Lawless, William Archbold and James Lawless were farmers, under the Crown, of Bray Manor. In 1368 Hugh Lawless was tried for unjustly ejecting William, son of Thomas Lawless, from the lands of Old Connaught.

King Edward III had granted the manors of Killruddery and Bray to the Archbold family. An Archbold of Killruddery is mentioned in 1385 and another in 1399, and the district became known as Archbold's country. They were of Anglo-Norman origin but to a certain degree had identified themselves with the Irish. However, the Fitzwilliams appear to have staked a claim on part of the town and made the Archbolds their tenants.

For over a century the state of war continued between the Norman and Irish tribes. In 1394 William Lawless was slain while protecting the frontiers of the Pale. The situation at the time required constant vigilance and, at her own expense, his widow Katherine FitzEustace maintained the men who had served under her husband at their posts.

In 1402, during the reign of King Henry IV, a fierce battle was fought near Ravenswell in which the septs and citizens of Dublin, headed by John Drake, Lord Mayor of Dublin, defeated a force of the O'Byrnes. According to Ware and Camden, 4,000 were slain but Henry de Marlbrigge put the total at 400. The battlefield became known as Bloody Bank. In honour of the occasion the Corporation of Dublin received the privilege of walking behind a gilt sword in procession.

In 1460 custody of the property of Walter Harold of Old Connaught was granted to John, son of Reginald Talbot. The castle of Old Court was built in 1440 by an English knight, Sir Thomas Mulso, who obtained a grant of land in what was then called the marshes of County Dublin on condition that he impose on the occupants a state of order and obedience to the Crown. He succeeded in taking possession of the land and building a castle, which he called Mulso's Castle (now Old Court Castle). Several expedi-tions assembled there to set out against the rebellious natives. One such army consisted of 1,100 men with provisions and machines for hurling stones. Mulso was killed soon afterwards in a skirmish and the castle passed into the hands of the Walshe clan of Carrickmines, some of whom held it until the rebellion of 1641. It was also the rendezvous from which one of Lord Deputy Russell's expeditions stated out against Fiaich McHugh O'Bryne in 1595.

Shanganagh Castle, 2 miles north of the town, was built a little earlier in the century by Thomas Lawless, who held the land for the vicars-choral of Saint Patrick's Cathedral, Dublin. The Lawless family was one of the town's principal landowners and also held lands on the site of an ancient abbey and burial place. The lands of Corke and Connaught, valued at £200, consisted of 500 acres, 400 of which were arable land, 50 were pastures and 50 meadow. The Walshe clan was later to take over areas of property that had been held by the Lawless clan.

A patent of Killruddery was granted to Sir William Brabazon by Henry VIII, along with two foot soldiers for the defence of the property, a feudal link with the defence of the country. He built Fassaroe and Powerscourt castles in 1535, which were handed over to Peter Talbot, a vigorous defender of the Pale, at the rent of 40 shillings per annum. The English found it impossible to suppress the Irish and in 1587 Aodh Ruadh O'Domhnaill, a young chief of Tyrconnell (now Donegal), was imprisoned for four years but escaped and spent an extremely cold winter evading capture in the Wicklow Mountains.

At the beginning of the fifteenth century the lands of Old Connaught, Corke and Shanganagh were owned by Aveline Lawless and later by Hugh Lawless. The lands of Ballyman passed from the Knights Templar into the possession of the Priory of Saint John of Jerusalem at Kilmainham in Dublin. In the sixteenth century all the lands in the parish of Old Connaught came into the possession of the Walshe family except those of Ballyman. After the Dissolution of the Monasteries by Henry VIII the lands of Old Connaught were granted to Peter Talbot. The Walshe family of Shanganagh was in possession of the lands of Old Connaught and Corke.

The barbaric manners and customs of the period are best illustrated in a pardon granted in 1566 to a number of inhabitants of the neighbourhood. This document stated that William Walshe of Corke, described as a 'gentleman', assisted by a 'kern', had robbed from an elderly Irish widow at Glencree a brass pan, two gallons of butter, a high-gown, two gowns and a cloak, for which offence Walshe had been arrested at Old Connaught by the sub-sheriff. As the latter was bringing his prisoner to Dublin he was set upon at Shanganagh and his prisoner taken from him by a number of neigh-bours, described as gentlemen, yeomen horsemen and kerns and including John Walsh of Shanganagh, James Goodman of Loughlinstown and Edmund Walshe of Corke. As the services of these people were too valuable to the Crown to be lost, the offence was treated as trivial and a free pardon was issued to all concerned. Immediately afterwards the principal offenders, John Walshe and James Goodman, were appointed commissioners for the muster of the militia. In Goodman, the English found a most active and determined enemy. Later, in depositions made by his neighbours, he was accused of cruelty and at least one murder, for which he was executed. His victim was a tenant of his own named William Boatson, and the murder was committed in a camp that the rebels had in Bray.

The Crown asserted its claim to the manor of Bray when in 1602 it seized 50 acres, and the following year claimed its right to the manor and proclaimed the Archbolds as trespassers. In 1611 Patrick Archbold, in making a petition for a search of his title to the Manor of Bray, claimed that his ancestors had held the manor for more than 200 years from the Earl of Ormond. They were unable to produce any deeds or records. The Fitzwilliams also made a claim to the Manor. This dispute was not settled finally until 1666 when a partition agreement was signed by the Earl of Meath. This title is now held by the Brabazon family.

After the rebellion of 1641 many English settlers were driven away and the lands within the parish came under the control of the Confederate Party. In depositions made after the Rebellion, William Pigeon of Ballyman related how, on coming down from the old castle, he was assaulted by 'three score lusty rebels' and forced to flee to Dublin. Frances Tuke, of Phrompstown, related that her servants were unable to protect her cattle and goods from raids by the insurgents. In the year following the rebellion, the neighbouring castle of Fassaroe was stormed and taken by the English and the cannons were removed. Subsequently one of the stations occupied by the Confederate troops was Much Bray, which by the end of the sixteenth century was regarded as one of the principal villages near Dublin. Its owners, the Archbolds, were regarded by the locals as men of integrity and distinction.

Following the establishment of the Commonwealth, the Walshe property in Old Connaught parish, including the lands of Old Connaught, Corke and part of Little Bray, were leased to Major Henry Jones but subsequently came, together with the other lands of the parish, into the possession of John Baxter. These other lands included Ballyman, which at the time of the rebellion belonged to Colonel Ponsonby, and the remainder of Little Bray was on land owned by the latter. At the end of the Commonwealth we find ten Irish inhabitants on the lands of Phrompstown; on the lands of Little Bray, eleven English and fifteen Irish; on the lands of Old Connaught, ten English and sixty-seven Irish (the main person being Edward Billingsley); and on the lands of Ballyman six English and thirty-one Irish (the chief person being Henry Bennett). The Fleetwood Survey of 1640 valued Old Connaught House at £20 and described it as a 'very fayre castle' consisting of a low building with a tower rising out of it near one end. Close by was the small town of Connaught with its church that was already a ruin. Although both church and chancel were in ruins, services were still held

there by the curate, Thomas Davis, who served the two churches of
Connaught and Kilmacanogue. Only fourteen poor labourers attended the
service. The rest of the people were all Roman Catholics and went to Mass
in the big house where Walshe maintained both friars and priests to attend
to their spiritual needs. Walshe also supported a teacher, Garret Warren,
who taught the local children.

In 1649 Oliver Cromwell sailed to Dublin with 9,000 infantry and 4,000
cavalry with instructions to subdue all opposition, extend the power of the
Crown in Ireland and to punish Catholics for the 1641 rising and their
alleged massacre of Ulster settlers. He first took Drogheda, County Louth,
and massacred the entire garrison of 3,500 Royalists. Following the
massacre Cromwell and his army marched south and destroyed Fassaroe
Castle as it passed through Bray. The Cromwellian Plantation caused two-
thirds of the land in Ireland to change hands and ended the activities of the
many rebel clans including the O'Tooles and the O'Byrnes. An Act of
Settlement passed in 1661 confirmed Cromwell's new settlers in their
holdings and at the same time any of the dispossessed who could prove that
they were innocent of any complicity in the Rising of 1641 were to be
reinstated.

The main reason for so much land agitation was that the country had
never been accurately mapped. In an attempt to rectify the situation, in
1654 Dr William Petty, an army physician, was offered the task of mapping
the entire country. Petty employed soldiers to do the actual measuring of
land and the result was a most accurate and complete set of maps for
Ireland. It became known as the Down Survey for the simple reason that
its findings were written down. The results for the Bray area were interesting – it showed the four main castles in the town, Little Bray and Old
Bray, together with Old Court to the south and Connaught (Connought)
to the west. Of this latter castle no trace is to be found. On a larger map
from the Survey Fassaroe Castle is clearly defined. It also shows a large
detached house on the west side of the street and at least two dwellings to
the south. This map shows Bray at an inaccurate 'IX miles' from Dublin –
in fact Bray is 12 statute miles from the city.

Until this period a major obstacle prevented Bray from becoming a large
settlement – the absence of a bridge between Counties Dublin and
Wicklow where the river had to be forded. This was a difficult operation
following heavy rain. The only other north–south route was over the
mountains. In 1666 permission was sought and granted for the erection of
a stone bridge and the work was carried out. Permission was also granted
at this time for the erection of tanpits for the tanning of leather but this
industry does not appear to have materialised.

In 1690, after the Battle of the Boyne, James II stayed for one night at
Puck Castle on the northern slope at Shankill. Early the next morning he

arrived in Bray and, learning that he was closely pursued, he posted a strong force at the bridge with instructions to remain until noon to block the passage of the pursuers. Fearing an ambush in the woods of Killruddery, James retreated and, seizing a boat on Killiney beach, sailed past Bray Head to Wicklow and eventually on to France.

In 1700 a barracks was built close to St Paul's Church with stones from de Ridelsford's Castle of Bray. The heavily fortified barracks, which could accommodate two companies of troops, put an end to the rebel raids on the town. The bridge, together with the ending of the raids, brought considerable growth and prosperity to the town. By the end of the seventeenth century there were forty-one dwellings in the town housing a population of 250.

3

GARRISON TOWN

By 1700 Bray was a medium-sized fishing and market town. The development of the town was largely attributable to its strategic location. It was also one of the most picturesque and conveniently situated towns in the country. Some problems did occur, as in 1741 when one end of the bridge was carried away in a fierce storm and the other end became so dangerous that there were fears the entire structure would be swept away. The bridge was quickly replaced by a sturdier structure with four arches. A map of Bray in 1762 by Jonathan Barker, commissioned by Lord Fitzwilliam, gives an indication of the size of the town centre. Starting at the bridge, it shows four large two-storey houses, the most southerly of which was detached. Immediately to the south of this house was a lane leading to the high ground overlooking Main Street where the castle of Bray, St Paul's Church and the barracks were all situated. To the south of the lane were four medium-sized dwellings and south of them five cabins and further south still, eight slightly larger cabins. All seventeen dwellings were owned by Lord Fitzwilliam, two being leased to Foster Adair of Killarney, eight to Joseph Smalley and seven to Doctor Lyons. All the dwellings were occupied by individual sub-tenants.

The poor of Little Bray lived in deplorable conditions. Their dwellings consisted in the main of single-room mud cabins with four walls of dried mud and a natural earth floor. The smallest of these cabins was about 12ft wide and between 12 and 20ft long. The roof consisted of sods of earth placed on wooden rafters and covered with a rough thatch. Most of these cabins had no windows or chimney and the smoke from the fire escaped through the open door or through a hole in the roof. Parents, children, sometimes even grandparents had to live, sleep and eat in one room. There was little furniture other than a primitive table, chairs and one bed, with the children usually sleeping on straw in a scooped-out hollow in the floor.

There were few cooking utensils – a pot, a container for carrying water from the well or stream and plates and mugs made of earthenware or wood. The diet of the poorer families was skimmed milk and potatoes that were eaten at most meals. Eggs, butter and fish were regarded as luxuries. Christmas was probably the only time at which they would eat meat. Local relief committees were formed to distribute free soup to destitute families. Many were given to poaching salmon and trout on the river to prevent starvation. Frequently children were sent in search of driftwood and twigs to kindle fires.

Clothing was of poor quality and most children went barefoot. Few labourers possessed an overcoat and they usually only wore a shirt, waistcoat and trousers repeatedly patched. Employees fortunate enough to be tenants or working for the more benevolent landlords like Lord Meath, the Plunkets or the Putlands, lived just above the poverty line. They and their families sometimes received cast-offs from the gentry. The average life span for an adult was forty-seven years and there was a high mortality rate amongst children. For many, employment was seasonal and irregular as they were only taken on to staff summer houses and hotels.

Lord Fitzwilliam began to lease large tracts of his Bray land in 1717 and registered deeds for these still exist. A significant document was the Religious Census of 1766 that showed 70 Protestant and 245 Catholic households – a total of 315 – in the three parishes, implying a population of 500–600. A labourer's wages were 10d per day in the summer but 8d in the winter owing to the shorter working day.

The houses had by now spread further along the Main Street as far the Poundhouse. At this juncture the road divided – the left and more important fork travelling through Delgany and Ashford on to Wicklow, the right fork travelling only a far as Kilmacanogue. Houses had also been built on Seapoint Road, which ran parallel to the river and was the only public way to the sea. Other dwellings were erected on the lane to the north of the barracks, on the lane leading to the mill at the south of the church, on one or two cul-de-sac lanes off the Main Street and a small number in Little Bray. In rural parts of the town some scattered dwellings had been erected. On the lands surrounding Old Court the village of Newtown-Vevay gradually developed.

Around this time there was a wide range of shops and trades in the town, and records show that by the mid-eighteenth century the following occupations were practised: grocers, butchers, victuallers, bakers, inn-keepers, millers, brewers, publicans, shoemakers, weavers, woollen drapers, saddlers, masons, carpenters, builders and wig-makers. The only industries known to exist at the beginning of the century had been brewing, distilling and milling. The brewery produced 300 barrels of beer and ale weekly. A guidebook said of the brewery 'Bray Ale is a celebrity and was regarded as being a neither bitter nor sweet ale but a combination of both which makes it exceedingly pleasant. The malting-floors, cooling-rooms, and vats are extensive and the greatest care is exercised in the mysteries of production.' Many residents living in close proximity to the mill complained of the constant noise from the machinery. Employees worked a sixty-hour week from 6 a.m. to 8.30 p.m. They had to work in confined spaces and there were fines for whistling or talking. Close to the mill was Watkins, Jameson and Pim & Co. (Maltings). It was not a distillery but a pre-processing operation to prepare the raw material for transport to Dublin for distilling. There is also evidence of a small woollen and linen industry and the garments they manufactured were distributed to the poor.

One flamboyant character living near Bray Common around this time was Richard, Earl of Anglesey, a defendant in the well-known Anglesey peerage case. His life in Bray, as disclosed after his death in proceedings before the House of Lords in London, with regard to fresh claims to his titles, was a source of great scandal. In 1741 he celebrated the victory of the British at Cartagena by distributing beer to soldiers and other residents of Bray.

The family name of Roberts appears in the middle of the eighteenth century as owners of the Walshe possessions at Shanganagh. The first of the Roberts family connected with Old Connaught was Lewis, the eldest son of an eminent doctor of law and Member of Parliament for Dungarvan, Dr Robert Roberts. Having obtained possession of the Old Connaught property, Lewis reclaimed the lands, although he does not appear to have resided there. The thanks and a gold medal from the Royal Dublin Society were voted to him for preserving some 38,000 trees that had been planted at Old Connaught in the previous 115 years. He was succeeded by his son John, who built Old Conna Hill House. In 1776 the Walshes' old residence, Old Connaught House, then occupied by Alderman Willoughtby Lightburne, was the scene of a disastrous fire, which entirely engulfed the house, although fortunately no lives were lost. Subsequently, in 1783, the land on which the house had stood was purchased by the Right Reverend William Gore, Bishop of Limerick, who rebuilt the residence but did not live to enjoy it as he died the following year.

Bray was connected to Dublin by a main road that ran through the town and on along the coastal route to Wicklow. By the 1770s coaches were running to and from Bray and in the next few decades the number of vehicles serving the Bray area rose steadily and their frequency was responsible for the town receiving three postal deliveries per week. Delgany and Enniskerry had no postal service at the time. Mail coaches were introduced to the county in 1790. One local coach owner, Tobias Toole, advertised journeys to all parts of the country.

Quin's Hotel, built in 1776 on the site of the present Royal Hotel, quickly gained a widespread reputation for good food, comfort and pleasant surroundings. It became increasingly common for tourists wishing to explore County Wicklow to make the hotel their base and to start excursions from there. John Quin, the proprietor, was so encouraged that he established a post-chaise service under the name of 'Quinbray' which was reputedly one of the best in Ireland. In 1787 Quin acquired an adjoining plot of waste ground known as Cock Walk (17 acres) from John Fury for 999 years; later deeds refer to this area as the place where the Bray Hotel was erected. The small original hotel building was extended onto the waste ground that stretched eastward to the sea and had a private path to the beach. Quin had the gardens landscaped with ornamental lawns on either side of this path and he became the largest landowner in Great Bray. Many travellers to County Wicklow mention Quin's Hotel in their journals.

The author William Makepeace Thackeray described its meals as the best in Ireland. The travel writer John Carr said it was the best hotel in the area. Mr and Mrs Hall in their travel journal *Ireland: Its scenery, its character* referred to it as the most splendid hotel in the kingdom. Another guide claimed that it was better than any service in England and stated: 'The hotel and posting house, conducted by Mr John Quin, is fitted up with every regard to the superior accommodation of families and visitors of the highest respectability; hot and cold sea water baths may be had at all hours without delay, and the house has long been a favourite resort of parties to spend the day in festivity and in enjoyment of the beauties of the surrounding scenery.' People travelling between Dublin and Wicklow in their own carriages frequently stayed a night in Quin's Hotel if they could afford it.

The proprietor permitted his friends in the town to look over the news-papers in the coffee room when they were not being read by the guests. The papers of the time were the *Dublin Evening Mail* which cost 5d, *The Nation* (a weekly paper) 6d, *Freeman's Journal* and *Saunders Newsletter*, which were dailies at 4d each.

The beauty spots of the county received widespread recognition when William Wilson named the sights to be included in the itineraries of any tourist: lakes, caves, mountains, waterfalls, glens, towers and ruined abbeys. He was one of the first to realise the enormous tourist potential of the county and highlighted the fact that within a short distance of Bray the visitor could visit Glendalough, Glencree, the Meeting of the Waters, Glen of the Downs, the Scalp, the Sugarloafs, Powerscourt demesne, Dargle Valley and the Devil's Glen. With this favourable publicity Bray was to gain the title 'Gateway to the Garden of Ireland'.

The first tourists hardly bothered to glance at the town on their way further south. One observer in 1800 claimed that architecturally Bray was more like an Indian township consisting of only 'a cluster of cabins'. The

unimpressive thatched cottages were the complete opposite of the fashionable image portrayed by the new residents and gentry living in houses
surrounding the town.

By the second half of the eighteenth century sea bathing had become a
popular pastime and many of the miraculous cures previously considered
the exclusive property of spa water were gradually being transferred to sea
water. Many visitors came to Bray to immerse themselves in the sea to cure
themselves of a variety of ailments which the experts claimed such an
exercise would overcome. Surgeon-Colonel Edgar Flinn, Medical
Inspector of the Irish Local Government Board, in his excellent work *Irish
Health Resorts and Watering Places*, stated:

> Bray possesses unusual attractions and has grown rapidly in popularity as a
> marine health resort of the first order. It has become one of the most
> bracing of our seaside places, and is naturally in great favour with the
> residents of the Metropolis. The air at Bray is bracing and invigorating and
> is especially suited to that class where there is debility and general loss of
> tone, induced by overwork or long illness or other depressing agencies.

During the summer months the town became extremely popular, with
visitors trekking along the steep, rough and winding Seapoint Road from
the town to the strand. Of course those who were fortunate enough to be
guests in Quin's Hotel could reach the sea by the private path in the
grounds.

As there was no fair-green, the May and September fairs were held on
the street where the old Courthouse now stands, and the activities extended
down as far as the castle in Little Bray. Booths and stalls were erected on the
side of the roadway from which farmers, fishermen and traders sold their
produce. The weekly Thursday markets were noisy, haphazard affairs
sprawling along the Main Street, causing disruption to traffic and annoyance
to the locals. Fairs and races in the area were colourful and bustling events
with jugglers, acrobats and hawkers in large numbers. On the Dublin side
of the river there was a race-track where races were held annually. Were it
not for the fashionable image of Quin's Hotel and the distinguished
residents on the outskirts, Bray would have been similar to any other small
county town of the period. Later markets held on Tuesdays and Saturdays
were abundantly supplied with provisions of the best quality. Fairs were held
quarterly and were attended by all the Dublin dealers. Periodic cattle sales
were also held in the town. The fair at Rathmichael had to be moved to
Carrickmines because of frequent bouts of faction-fighting. The last
recorded faction-fight in Bray took place at Ravenswell Gate when a
gentleman of small stature dispersed the participants with only a riding crop.
Occasional duels were not unknown in the locality.

The harbour at the mouth of the river was little more than an anchorage and the low-lying area inland from it was repeatedly flooded. In 1787 a channel was cut, which made the river navigable, but the operation had to be repeated annually due to heavy silting. During most of the year small craft carrying coal, slate and limestone landed their cargo at a small dock on the southern bank below Seapoint Road. Grain and timber were exported from the dock.

Around this time there was only heaped sand, low sand dunes and shingle along the shoreline, with a rough raised pathway leading to Bray Head. Numerous hollows and irregularities were created in the ground by the digging and carting away of sand by farmers and others in the locality. There were then only two habitations on the seafront. In one, a small, attractive cottage where the Bray Head Hotel now stands, lived an elderly woman and her daughters. They made their livelihood from selling pebbles from the beach known as Wicklow pebbles and beach-combing the strand for shipwrecked goods. The second dwelling, a mud hovel, known locally as 'The Rat Hole', was the home of an eccentric, solitary old fisherman, who surrounded his abode with ill-smelling heaps of manure, offal and seaweed. Goats and donkeys roamed freely on the open space.

In the latter part of the eighteenth century Bray became associated with smuggling. The wild and desolate coast around Bray Head offered many facilities to the smugglers. Corruption was rife among Revenue officers, who frequently accepted bribes, and on the whole, the authorities failed to curb the practice. The most successful plan adopted by the smugglers was to send their contraband goods ashore in boats, under cover of darkness or in misty weather, to pre-arranged places of concealment along the coast and then to sail openly onwards with their legitimate cargo to Dublin or other ports.

The best-known landing place was a cave about half a mile along the Cliff Walk – known appropriately as the Brandy Hole – where smugglers discharged their cargo into numerous receptacles left for that purpose. Over this cavern and adjoining the rough track then encircling the Head was a shaft sunk in a slanting direction into the earth, linked with another subterranean chamber, but no trace could be seen from the top as the entrance was carefully concealed by thick branches. Contraband was hauled up by means of a rope and pulley. From 1760 reports of seizures of brandy, tea and silk were quite common. Raithin a' Chluig was one of the locations for concealing these cargoes.

During the war of 1778–83 there were stories of pirate cutters being sighted in the area. One report tells of a pirate vessel with twenty guns being launched on Bray strand amid the loud acclamation of local people, all clamouring to go on board. As a means of ending this illicit trade customs officers were installed in a coastguard station near the present Bray Head Hotel.

Henry Grattan's acquaintance with Bray began long before he came to live there; in fact he had loved that part of Wicklow all his life. In 1770 he wrote from London to a friend about the 'romantic valley' where he afterwards lived. In 1779, when he and his colleagues were determined to add an amendment dealing with the export trade of Ireland to the address of the lord lieutenant, Grattan, Dennis Daly and Burgh agreed to meet at Bray and discuss the subject. As they sat on the seashore Daly became ill and had to depart but not before he had drawn up a statement that he gave to Grattan. Grattan was greatly impressed by Daly's ability and strongly believed that had he lived to the end of the century there would have been no 1798 Rebellion.

Grattan represented Dublin in the British House of Commons from 1800 until his death. Parliament voted that £100,000 should be given to Grattan as a reward for his services but it was with difficulty that he was persuaded to accept half that amount. With the payment he bought Tinnehinch, a fine house, a few miles west of Bray, on the banks of the Dargle. He lived there from the end of 1782 – not only the year of his greatest fame but also the year of his marriage.

During the 1798 Rebellion the United Irishmen and the government were both anxious that Grattan's name should be amongst the insurgents. On one occasion during Grattan's absence some yeomen called to his house and stated that they had proof of his treason and 'the plan he had taken of the Dargle'. Lord Powerscourt ordered the soldiers not to molest Mrs Grattan but they destroyed the orchard at Tinnehinch. Following the Battle of Arklow soldiers stopped at the house and some of the group proposed blowing it up but the majority were against doing so. After the Union Grattan retired to Tinnehinch and gave himself up to study and the education of his children until he died in May 1820.

Other members of the Irish Parliament owning town houses near Bray around this period were George Rawson, MP for the Borough of Armagh, who had a house at Belmont; Sir Francis Hutchinson, MP for the Borough of Jamestown, County Leitrim, who lived at Old Conna and later moved to Palermo House and was High Sheriff of Dublin in 1783; and George Roth, MP for the Borough of Thomastown, who lived at Fairview, Bray. Sir William Hawkins, Ulster King-of-Arms resided at Bolton Hall; the Right Honourable Theophilus Jones lived at Corke Abbey; and the Right Honourable John Monck Mason, an uncle of the historian of St Patrick's Cathedral and himself an author and politician, resided at Thornhill.

The Rathdown Cavalry, under the command of Captain Edwards of Old Court, headed the procession from the Royal Exchange to the Rotunda when the famous meeting of the Irish Volunteers took place on 10 November 1783. Lord Powerscourt (third Viscount) was commander of the Wicklow Volunteers. The cavalry were drilled on the commons where the

Bray races were later held. The rebellion of 1798 inevitably affected the town since it was geographically close to the most troubled areas of south Wicklow and Wexford. At the time there were only two garrisons in the county, one in Bray and one in Wicklow. For the rest they relied on the local yeomen, scattered in small detachments over the bogs and mountains. Bray had a military barracks and hospital and many wounded were transferred there although the town itself was not involved in the fighting to any large degree due to the efforts of Captain Edwards. His liberal-mindedness and understanding of the situation – traits both highly individualistic and at the same time characteristic of the attitude of the area – were to prevent the upsurge of ill-feeling which pushed the rest of the county into revolt.

Captain Edwards was a local magistrate and commander of the Bray yeomanry corps and an ex-volunteer. From March 1798 his liberal opinions had brought him to the attention of the government that was being pressurised by twenty-eight other magistrates who attacked the Bray Infantry as 'a hotbed of traitors'. Under strong pressure the government agreed to the purging of more than a hundred men from five corps, including Bray. Intelligence reports reaching Dublin Castle indicated that Wicklow was 'extensively and formidably organised' and had mustered a force of 12,000 men.

Early in 1798 the garrison commander, Major Joseph Hardy, reported that a religious revolt was impending in south Wicklow. In May 1798, following the introduction of a brutal policy of forcible disarmament accompanied by atrocities in other areas, Major Hardy requested Captain Edwards to send reinforcements. Edwards refused to send his troops to assist in this campaign and declined to enforce the policy in the Bray area. Edwards stated, 'I deprecate dragooning such people – it is a bad system except in open rebellion. Where is the man whose blood will not boil with revenge who sees the petticoat of his wife or sister cut off her back by the sabre of the dragoons – merely for the crime of being green, a colour certainly with them innocent of disaffection.' He had been for eighteen years a magistrate among these people and had pledged himself to protect them from outrage as long as they observed the law. He threw down this challenge to Major Hardy: 'If the troops come to Bray and commit outrages under the semblance of law I will use every means to punish them.'

In Bray Edwards was prepared to accept surrender without forced disarmament and to offer free pardon without conditions of giving information. As a result of this action he was relieved of his duties and his corps dismissed, having earned for himself a reputation as a 'temporising magistrate'. Before troops could be despatched to Bray to forcibly disarm its inhabitants the rebellion had broken out on 20 May. From the outset the town was quiet, tensions undoubtedly eased by the fair policy of Captain Edwards.

There were a number of major incidents in the district – on 8 June an innkeeper in the town was arrested as a spy and on 17 July several boys employed in the brewery beside the bridge ran away to join the insurrection, having received orders from their commander. A Sergeant Ledwidge and a Corporal Kennedy were executed as traitors in the area. Sir Edward Crosbie, who lived in Bray, was also executed in 1798. His father, Sir Paul, had been barrack-master of the town. On the night of 7 June the town received news that rebels were approaching from the Killruddery direction but despite an all-night vigil by troops there was no attack. A report which reached the *Freeman's Journal* in July 1793 of rebel troops being quartered in the town and the townspeople refusing to support the militia was certainly unfounded. At no time during the crisis was any loyalist of the area injured or threatened, a testament to the good relations in the district. During the worst of the troubles of 1799, at the time when the parish priest of Arklow was shot dead in his bed, the parish priest of Bray was given refuge in the house of the Earl of Meath and was granted permission to say mass there. The Earl endeavoured to avoid any hostilities in the town and the murder of the parish priest would have inevitably brought serious repercussions.

4

CHANGING TIMES

In 1793, when Britain was at war with Napoleon's France, the British government raised a militia of 20,000 men in Ireland. The officer commanding in each county could enforce conscription but men of substance were able to insure themselves against this. There was imminent danger of a French invasion of Ireland and Dublin Bay was considered to be most vulnerable. Killiney beach was considered to be one of the most strategic places for a landing and the government established a large military camp in nearby Loughlinstown in 1795. As a further precaution, the British government ordered that thirty towers and batteries be erected along the coastline from Bray to Balbriggan as watchtowers in the event of an invasion.

These were called Martello Towers, a term originating from a similar tower at Cap Martello in Corsica. They were designed to be erected in sight of each other so that on viewing an approaching enemy fleet a message could be relayed from tower to tower back to army headquarters in Dublin. Three of these towers were constructed on the coastline at Bray in 1804, the first on a sandbank near Bray Head close to where the boat house new stands. The second is still standing near the harbour and has been converted into a dwelling. The third was situated at Corke Abbey and has long since disappeared. A report in the *Dublin Builder* magazine on 18 November 1864 stated that this tower had been found to be shaky and unsafe, having been undermined by the sea at high tides. These circular towers, about 30ft high, were constructed of carefully cut granite and were generally of a standard design with only minor modifications. Their usual armament was a 24-pounder gun on a traversing platform. As a security precaution the door faced away from the sea and was about ten feet above ground level. The towers were situated between ½ mile and 1½ miles apart to give mutual support with an overlapping field of fire from the guns. The main intention was to delay or obstruct a landing on the beaches. Each tower, costing approximately £1,800, was manned by a small garrison and made the maintenance of small local barracks superfluous, although military opinion at the time was divided as to the effectiveness of the gun towers for coastal defence. At the same time new roads were constructed on which the military could move quickly. They were designed to connect outlying areas to Dublin. In the Returns of Barracks of Ireland for 1811 the complement of the Bray Barracks was given as three officers and sixty-four infantry.

At the beginning of the nineteenth century there were complaints about the general condition of the roads in the area. One observer noted that where once the roads of the town were noted for their excellent condition, they had now fallen into disrepair. A local magistrate, Justice Day, complained of the near impossibility of carrying out his duties due to the deplorable state of the roads. The most dangerous area was reputedly the steep hill from the bridge into Little Bray through the street called Back Street, which was extremely narrow. A local landowner, John Donnellan, donated a stretch of land to the east of Back Street on which Castle Street was built – this then became the main through road to Dublin.

To repair the remainder of the roads would have proven a costly and difficult operation and steps were taken to raise revenue by erecting turnpikes on several approach roads to Bray. These were the equivalent of today's toll roads. There was strong opposition from the community and many protest meetings were held. In 1811 a new mail coach route was inaugurated linking Dublin with Wicklow and Wexford, passing through Bray, the one place where the Dargle was bridged at the time. The only road southwards went via Windgates to Delgany on through Kilcoole and then to Ashford. The authorities decided to open a more direct route through the Glen of the Downs. The road was completed in 1814. The following year a new coach – the *Waterloo* – travelling as far as Waterford was initiated and used the new road. The journey from Dublin to Wicklow took five and a half hours, with coaches setting out at 6 a.m., breakfasting in Bray and arriving in Wicklow about 11.30 a.m. The fare from Dublin to Bray was 3s 9d if the passengers travelled inside, 2s 6d if they travelled outside with the baggage, with no guarantee against accidents or damage to property. In 1815 a new line for the mail-coach was opened between Dublin and Bray, running through Blackrock and Kill-of-the-Grange and meeting the older road that ran through Stillorgan.

With the mail coaches passing through Bray it was decided to erect a turnpike at Violet Hill. Only at this stage did the people of the town begin to reconsider their opposition to the road system and turnpike charges in the area. One major advantage of the better roads was that communications greatly improved, a point that had been overlooked by the previous protesters. By 1832, when the committee of turnpikes made its report, locals decided that rather than cause further disruptions they would suffer the inconvenience and expense of the system.

Many jarveys operated in the town and the oldest name connected with the business was Traynor, whose family firm dated from 1840. There was a renowned jarvey nicknamed the 'Bit of Cake', who on one occasion deserted his cab at a public house in Kilmacanogue on a return journey from Glendalough leaving his fares to drive themselves home in the dark. A master carman, with the appropriate name of Carr, employed several drivers while Christy Leonard and his brother, infamous for their mispronunciation, also carried passengers around Bray and its environs. Best value of all was with Tony Miles who ran his own service and charged a shilling for a trip around the town with the added bonus of minding the children while their parents went shopping.

One of the oldest shops in the town was The Mart, run by Thomas Miller, who was noted for his first-rate material. From the middle of the century he had a rival in the millinery department when Mrs McDonald opened her establishment on the opposite side of the street, but when Quinsboro Road was opened she took the corner shop facing Quin's Hotel. Her material was rated so highly that many customers travelled out from Dublin even in the winter to buy her merchandise. Next to Navarre Gate a Mr Devereux ran a shoemaker's shop and close to the weir in the 'Valley of Diamonds' a tailor named Broderick made suits for the gentry.

Packmen flourished at this time, selling linen and silk for ladies' dresses. The Putland family employed forty women in the manufacture of flax and wool. A wealthy family named Hodsons bequeathed the Adair Fund worth £60 per annum to the poor of Bray and the same sum to the poor in the parishes of Delgany and Powerscourt. Some enterprising women set up an industry to make women's nightcaps for sale in Dublin.

This industry flourished until the 1860s, when night-caps went out of vogue. Eight-day clocks, which appear to have been in almost every house, were attended to by an itinerant clock-maker. He walked in as soon as the door was opened and if the clock was working looked at it and walked out remarking 'wonderful old clock'. There were no fishmonger shops; fish was sold in baskets and barrows in the streets. Fruit was also sold from baskets but none of the gentry sold fruit or vegetables from their gardens. Sugar-sticks and other sweets were offered for sale at street corners. The local chimney sweep was named Lenihan and horses were shod by a man named Smith in Little Bray, who had an iron hook instead of a hand, which he lost in the Battle of Waterloo, gaining him the nick-name 'Iron Fist'. Sutton's of the Golden Ball and Kennedy's of Cabinteely supplied bread. Salmon and trout fishing in the Bray River were a profitable business.

From the end of the eighteenth century many distinguished politicians and professional men came to live in the manors on the outskirts of the town. Lord William Plunket, the first Baron Plunket, lived in Old Connaught House. In 1787 he was called to the bar and later defended the United Irishmen. In 1798 he was returned as MP for Charlemont. A friend of Wolfe Tone, he was appointed Solicitor-General and was prosecutor at the trial of Robert Emmet. He entertained many important figures at his home including Henry Grattan, Archbishop Magee of Dublin and many members of the judiciary. As Attorney-General in 1825 he was host to Sir Walter Scott in Bray. Raised to the peerage, Plunket was Lord Chancellor from 1830 until his resignation. Three of his children, none of whom supported his stand on Catholic relief, were prominent members of the Church of Ireland: one son was Bishop of Tuam and Killala, one was Dean of Tuam and one Vicar of Bray. Plunket died in 1854. His grandson, also William Plunket, resided in Old Connaught House. Following his marriage to Anne, the daughter of Sir Benjamin Lee Guinness, one of the founders of the brewing company, William was appointed a curate to St Patrick's Cathedral. Thereafter he had a speedy rise through the ranks of the church and was appointed Bishop of Meath and later Archbishop of Dublin. From Old Connaught he frequently called on Father James Healy, the well-known Catholic priest in Little Bray, and they walked together to the station to catch the train to Dublin.

Another important resident around that time was Charles Putland, who lived at Sans Souci with its cast iron conservatory (later called Newcourt House, now Loreto Convent). Both he and Lord Plunket were particularly benevolent to the poor and needy.

In 1893 when workmen were digging on Lord Plunket's estate they discovered a moat immediately inside the grounds opposite the entrance to Woodbrook. Lord Plunket contact the antiquarian W.K. Wakeman who later wrote two articles entitled *On a recently discovered Pagan Sepulchral Mound in the grounds of Old Connaught*. Five skeletons were found in the moat along with bones of cattle, deer, goats and pigs split open for the marrow, which would suggest a great funeral feast. Other items found included shells for necklaces, bronze food containers and, most interesting of all, two small stone slabs with markings that unfortunately proved impossible to decipher. After Archbishop Plunket's death in 1897, Old Connaught was let to different tenants, one of whom ran a girls' school there.

Politically there was little anti-imperialist feeling in Bray, mainly due to the resident landlords having a liberal and fair-minded attitude. The abdication of Napoleon in 1814 and visits by royalty and the lord lieutenant were received with enthusiasm. The Catholic Emancipation campaign generally met with approval as did the later Repeal Campaign.

According to the Census of Ireland in 1821, in the sixty years between 1761 and 1821 the number of houses in the Bray area increased from approximately 100 to 605. The total population increased by 1,110 with more than a third working in agriculture. Another third were employed in trade and manufacturing, but over the following twenty years the number of people engaged in this kind of work in Bray town and Little Bray increased by 30 per cent. In the same period the population of the area rose from 3,300 to 4,200.

From the mid-1830s the castle in Little Bray was used as a barracks for the constabulary and petty sessions were held there every alternate Saturday until the Courthouse was built in 1841. The Earl of Meath, as Lord of the Manor of Kindlestown, held court there through his seneschal every month. Later the Little Bray castle was rented by a butcher named Gerity.

The Ordnance Survey Report of 1839 stated that land rents in the town were high, ranging from £10 to £12 per acre, and the rural land around the town averaged £6 per acre. In the 1840s the houses in the Bray area were valued and classified under the Griffith Poor Law Valuation. The records of the estimators would tend to confirm that the majority of the dwellings in Bray parish and Little Bray were small, unimpressive cabins of low value, though in good repair and neatly kept. Very poor dwellings were not given a valuation, but of those listed over two-thirds were valued at under £5 and more than three-quarters were classified as medium. In the middle of the century almost half of the town's inhabitants could neither read nor write and in a list of the educational standards of 141 towns, Bray was number 64.

The famine years were to test the tenacity of the town, but the worst effects were offset by the co-operation and benevolence of the more fortunate inhabitants. Towards the end of October 1845 the first signs of failure of the potato crop became obvious. Fortunately the first winter was to pass without apparent hardship, but the following year the price of potatoes was noticeably higher in Bray. In April, forty men seeking employment from Loughlinstown Poor Law Guardians were turned away. As the winter of 1846 set in, distress was widespread, with storms raging and destroying fishermen's cottages in Dock Terrace and preventing fish catches from being landed to alleviate starvation. In January a survey indicated that of 2,383 men employed on the public works in County Wicklow only 170 were from Bray and of those thirty-six were made redundant with the advent of spring in March 1847. In August, work commenced on the railway at Bray Head and about 500 men were employed on it. Throughout the worst of the famine the needy of Bray were supplied with food and clothing by the local gentry and nobility. Lady Plunket set up soup kitchens whilst her husband increased his labourers' wages from 10s to 12s for a sixty-hour week to meet rising prices. Lady Meath and Mrs Putland distributed food and clothing to the poorest families. Crowds of beggars constantly waylaid Mrs Putland at the gate of Sans Souci when her carriage passed in and out. Mr Putland offered employment to destitute labourers and had the Putland Road built as a famine relief scheme.

There were fewer resident landlords in the west of Ireland so naturally there was more charity available in the east coast areas like Bray, where the resident gentry did provide considerable, if still inadequate, relief. Despite the efforts of these people Bray did suffer during the famine. The actual number of deaths is not known but there is evidence that the number was high. Records of burials for the Church of Ireland showed an average of eight deaths a year in the decade before the famine and ten in the decade after 1850, but an average of sixteen deaths per year in the five years between 1845 and 1850. Unfortunately no such records are available for the deaths of Roman Catholics. However, in 1841 there were 1,123 people living in the hinterlands of Bray and a decade later this had decreased to 799.

Dispensary services rendered were minimal but had they not existed during the famine years the consequences would have been far worse. From the 1830s onwards, due to overcrowding and ignorance about hygiene, the town experienced many cholera and smallpox epidemics, which led a doctor to report that 80 per cent of the houses had inadequate sewerage. In November 1833 an outbreak of cholera killed twenty-five people in Bray. When cholera struck again in 1876 Doctor Christopher Thompson, who resided at Duncairn Terrace, volunteered to look after the dying. He contracted the disease himself and died on 16 December that year and is buried in St Paul's Graveyard. On 26 January 1877 at a meeting in Quin's Hotel it was proposed to erect a memorial to his memory as a testimony of the high regard in which he was held by the people of Bray. This monument, in the form of an obelisk, can still be seen opposite St Paul's Church at the Royal Hotel.

In the Regency period the practice of sea bathing, and seaside resorts acquired a new aura of respectability and popularity, initiated by the royal residence at Brighton. Almost overnight, the Prince Regent's patronage erased the image of the seaside as just a place for invalids; instead there emerged amongst the upper classes an eagerness to be seen at the seaside. This trend gradually affected Bray and increasingly in the 1830s people of position and rank frequented the resort. From 1815 onwards jaunting cars brought day-trippers from Dublin leaving the city at 11 a.m. and returning from Bray at 6 p.m. for a return fare of half a crown. Owners of cottages began to lease their dwellings and lodging for the summer season. In 1837 an observer wrote: 'Thatched cottages of neatness from three to eight rooms each are let furnished for £40 to £50 and more for the season.' He also noted that some houses fetched as much as £100 for the season.

Many lawyers and judges resided in the town over the summer months, most notable amongst whom were Chief Justice Whiteside, Judge Keogh, Lord Ashbourne and Judge Lawson. The prestige of their residency affected the growth of Bray not only as a seasonal resort and starting point for excursions into the country but also as a centre for permanent fashionable residents. These developments took place outside the immediate town area, in developments such as Corke Abbey, built by William Morrison. Tinnehinch was converted from an old inn into a spacious residence by Henry Grattan, and Killruddery House, at the foot of the Little Sugarloaf, was refurbished in 1820 for the Earl of Meath. Other impressive buildings of this period included Woodbrook, Hollybrook, Fairy Hill, Violet Hill, Richview, Brayview and Edenview, the latter three built by Sir Sidney Herbert specifically as lodges to lease for the season. Killruddery House and Holybrook were Morrison designs. The names of Fassaroe and Vallambrossa were applied to several different houses over a span of time. The custom of giving French and Italian names to local places became common practice in Bray from the beginning of the nineteenth century. The occupants of these houses strove to maintain a cultural existence; they indulged in hunting, music and dancing, as well as attending a new theatre established at St Valerie's, beside the Dargle on the outskirts of the town.

5

THE COMING OF
THE RAILWAY

On 8 July 1854 the first train from Dublin arrived in Bray Station, carrying the directors of the railway company. Tea was served on the platform and in the evening a dance was held to the accompaniment of a military band. Two days later the railway was officially opened to the public. It was a quiet, uneventful day with a brief notice in the newspapers stating that 'the railway is opened in Bray from this day' the only testament to the occasion. This ceremony was in fact the result of almost twenty years of negotiating, planning and construction.

In 1833 when the country's first railway line from Dublin to Kingstown was being planned it was suggested the line should be extended to Bray. The following year, when Charles Vignoles was called upon to submit plans to the Dublin and Kingstown Railway Company for the Salthill–Dalkey extension, he was requested to continue his survey as far as Bray. A committee was appointed in 1837 to report on the advantages of running a line to Bray. In 1844 Isambard Kingdom Brunel, one of the world's leading engineers, visited the atmospheric railway which ran from Kingstown to Dalkey. He mentioned to the directors of the Dublin and Kingstown Railway that his own English company, the Great Western and South Wales, planned to build a line into South Wales and start a new steamer service from Fishguard to what is now Rosslare. He also envisaged a connecting railway from Wexford to Dublin and he suggested that the Dublin and Kingstown Railway might consider a joint venture. A plan to build an inland route through Bray to Wicklow and the south had always been considered. After some time the Great Western Railway's enthusiasm waned and the Dublin and Kingstown Railway decided to promote the Kingstown to Bray line on its own.

After a great deal of discussion and negotiations the Dublin–Kingstown Railway company realised that if a line to Bray was to become a reality it would have to be as an extension of the Dublin/Kingstown line, and Vignoles was requested to submit plans. He believed that there were three routes suitable for survey:

1. Dalkey–Bray with branches to Bray Head and Enniskerry
2. Blackrock–Shanganagh–Bray with same branches
3. Kingstown–Killiney–Bray

There was strong opposition in the Killiney area and Vignoles himself recommended consideration of the inland route via Blackrock and Shanganagh with the existing Dublin–Blackrock stretch being rebuilt on a wider gauge. Eventually more ambitious plans were formalised and a new company was set up to establish a line from Dublin to Wicklow and on to Wexford. In May 1845 the company known as the Wicklow, Wexford, Waterford and Dundrum & Dublin Railway Company, generally known as the 'Three Ws', was set up. Three months later work commenced, with a sod-cutting ceremony at Bray Head. Construction of the line began on 28 August 1847.

The plans for tunnelling under Bray Head were drafted by Brunel who stated that an expensive tunnel would have to be built through the Head as it was impossible to go round it. Many contractors and up to 500 men were employed on this segment of the scheme. Brunel's finished plans provided for only two short tunnels. The economic depression of the famine years and the company's internal problems made the progress extremely slow. In 1851 the company officially modified its enormous programme, changed its name to the Dublin and Wicklow Railway and abandoned the line from Dundrum to Rathfarnham. At the same time the Dublin and Kingstown Railway changed its name to the Dublin and Bray Railway. The Wicklow line was now set to run from St Stephen's Green to Dundrum and Shanganagh, meeting the Dublin and Bray line there and travelling on it as far as Bray, and continuing to Wicklow from Bray on the track made by the Dublin and Wicklow Railway. Construction on the Bray–Wicklow section proved a difficult feat of engineering. The first 5 miles along the sea cliffs involved three tunnels and four wooden trestle viaducts, while between Greystones and Wicklow the line was built along the edge of the foreshore. Due to various problems with coastal erosion, sharp curves, rock falls and accidents, four diversions had to be made in the subsequent sixty-three years, in 1876, 1879, 1888 and 1917, before the line took up its present position. It now has seven tunnels and one bridge. One of the original diversions was eventually by-passed itself so that there are short sections where three different lines have been laid. On this stretch there are also two under-bridges. Three of the original bridges were of timber, built to one of Brunel's characteristic designs. They were smaller versions of Brunel's larger bridges that he had constructed throughout south-west England. Stone piers were topped with timber that fanned out from the tops of the piers to support the horizontal timber beams. Only the stone piers remain today.

The route for the railway around Bray Head, with all its problems, seemed a strange choice to come from such an eminent and experienced engineer as Brunel, but the Earl of Meath did not want the railway to go through Killruddery and gave the Bray Head route free of charge. It was originally intended to have a double track through Bray Head and, although only one line was laid, the three original tunnels were built for a double track. The blasting of the tunnel was expensive but some revenue was recouped by selling the broken stones for road-making to contractors and public bodies. Robert Worthington, later a prominent railway contractor, had a quarry at Bray Head with a siding at his crushing and grading plant.

When William Dargan became involved in the project many problems still existed. Dargan was born in Carlow in 1799 and trained as an engineer and surveyor with Thomas Telford in Holyhead. In Ireland he worked on the Howth Road and the Grand and Ulster Canal projects. Winning the contract for the Dublin and Kingstown Railway brought him great prominence and he went on to become involved in almost every railway in the country. Dargan's connections with these companies were such that he often accepted shares as payment, thus becoming involved in the actual management of the railway. He always had a liking for Bray and brought his influence to bear in bringing the railway to the town.

Dargan bought out the English shares in the Dublin and Wicklow Railway and transformed the company into an Irish concern. He became a director and later chairman. Immediately he set about completing the line to Bray. He reached an agreement with the Dublin and Bray company whereby whichever company finished the line to Bray should take over the unfinished work of the other. The Dublin and Wicklow company, with Dargan in charge, won the race, working rapidly and employing large numbers of labourers and completing the Dundrum–Bray line in July. Towards the end of 1853 the Dublin–Dundrum section of the line was completed and Dargan then began to prepare the coastal route for through traffic. The Dalkey–Bray line was completed first, then the atmospheric between Dalkey and Kingstown, and finally the Kingstown–Dublin line was converted to the wider gauge. On 11 October 1853 the Dublin, Wicklow and Bray lines were joined. Dargan mediated between the groups and even bought a large number of Dublin and Wicklow shares. His considerable energy and dedication helped to speed up the construction. Finally, on 10 July 1854, the Dublin–Wicklow Railway opened for business between a temporary station at Harcourt Road and Bray, along with the

Dalkey to Bray section. The permanent terminus at Harcourt Street opened on 7 February 1855.

Bray station was a long classical building with dormer windows protected by a slanting roof, which was supported by a number of iron pillars. The broad extensive platforms on either side of the line were sometimes turned into a fashionable promenade when bad weather drove the band across from the gardens of Breslin's Marine Hotel. The station had well-arranged waiting rooms, and a first and second class centre for refreshments.

The next development should have been the automatic merger of the Dublin and Wicklow Railway and the Dublin and Kingstown Railway, but there were problems. The route through Bray Head, Brunel's work, was already showing deficiencies and relations between the companies deteriorated. In October 1855, with the opening of the new converted atmospheric railway, the Dublin and Wicklow Railway sent an abrupt letter to the Kingstown company announcing that it required the use of its station there and had therefore erected a booking office on the platform. The Dublin and Kingstown Railway was annoyed and on several occasions evicted the clerk and refused to allow passengers from Bray to alight at the station. This impasse continued for several days but normal relations were soon restored and on 1 July 1856 the Dublin and Kingstown Railway formally handed over its line to the Dublin and Wicklow Railway, having postponed the lease as long as possible. From that date all services were operated by the Dublin and Wicklow Railway although the Dublin and Kingstown Railway retained ownership of the line.

In July 1856, two years after the Bray and Wicklow extension opened, the long-awaited merger between the Dublin and Kingstown Railway and Dublin and Wicklow Railway took effect. The inland route was by Ranelagh, Dundrum and Shankill. This line was far less profitable than the Dublin and Kingstown Railway section and before long fares were increased to meet the deficit. There was a vast decline in the number of passengers travelling on the service with the higher fares leading to customer resistance and the revival of old forms of competition. The Dublin and Dundrum company protested that its line was being penalised for the inadequacy of the controlling company with high fares, poor services and infrequent connections. Many of the problems of the Dublin and Wicklow company can be traced to the construction of the other line so near to the seashore. It was unable to withstand winter storms and heavy seas despite the many short tunnels designed to protect the most exposed sections, and in time this became known as 'Brunel's Folly'. The original course of the line can clearly be seen from the Cliff Walk that runs parallel with the railway to Greystones. One curious aspect of the line was the camouflaged smoke vent that opened out on Bray Head itself and from where a gust of smoke would ascend from the ground as the train passed beneath.

A few weeks after the opening, traffic was temporarily stopped by a fall of clay at Morris's Cliffs at the southern end. There were also falls at Bray Head of rock from above the line, where the strata had been disturbed. The company had to arrange for constant watching. It soon became the rule to have three men on patrol all day, and two or three during the night.

In March 1857, only seventeen months after the line was opened, heavy falls of rock occurred and the line had to be shifted by 8–10ft at that place. Anxiety about the safety of the line around Bray Head was tragically justified. On 9 August 1867 the engine, tender and three carriages of the Enniscorthy–Dublin train left the track as it ran onto Number Two viaduct, south of Brabazon Tunnel, broke through the left-hand guard rail, and fell 33ft from the bridge. A Mr Murphy was killed and another passenger, Mrs Hackman, died later from her injuries. Fortunately the train landed on the inner side or casualties would have been higher. The rescue operation was extremely difficult and the injured were lifted into dropside mineral wagons, transferred to Shankill, and conveyed across a field to the workhouse at Loughlinstown. The engine and tender were not lifted for three weeks. The cause of the accident was a faulty joint in the rails and, as the inquiry found, 'the wretched manner in which the line was being relaid'. Despite evidence of poor maintenance and faulty construction, along with attempts to improve the line just before the inquiry, there was no public outcry against the company. The line was repaired and strengthened in parts and services resumed. It was not until 1912 that a decision was taken on full diversions for the troublesome sections.

In 1860 a proposal had been put forward for a steam railway service to link Bray and Enniskerry. Nothing materialised on the project until 1866 when an Act of Parliament was passed which gave parliamentary approval to construct the Bray and Enniskerry Light Railway. Work commenced in April 1891 but the scheme was bitterly opposed by the Bray town commissioners and Wicklow County Council until eventually the county council directed workmen to tear up the tracks. In 1893 the rails and sleepers were sold under a court judgement.

In 1900 the commissioners proposed trams for Bray and intended to connect this system with the Bray and Enniskerry line. Around this period there were schemes for tramways in various parts of Wicklow, including Enniskerry to Hollybrook, Glendalough to Hollybrook, and Dundrum to Enniskerry and Bray. None of these were built and the company was dissolved in 1901.

The arrival of the railway marked the beginning of a new prosperous era for Bray, with the advantage of easy access from Dublin and the terminus for steamers crossing the Irish Sea at Kingstown. When the line opened there were seven train services on the inland route and five on the coastal route. In 1856 eleven trains per day were running on the inland route and the following year it had increased to twenty-eight trains daily. The service was advertised as suitable for holidays by the sea and for people with business in the city. There was also a boost given to Bray as a tourist centre as areas boasting a railway in the vicinity automatically rose in status and popularity.

There was a conscious effort made by the company to promote and encourage tourism with dual benefit to the town and the company. They offered a variety of attractive deals: cheap excursion fares on Sunday and bank holidays, package deals including a day's fishing, family deals, dinner at a hotel in Bray, fairs, races, regattas and agricultural shows sponsored by the railway. They also erected bathing boxes for the use of visitors, employed military bands to play on the seafront and provided extra trains at difficult hours for special occasions. They launched promotion campaigns throughout Ireland and in England. The railway company became the most profitable in Ireland, being particularly successful in its cheap excursion fares programme: for example, on 2 April 1861, 4,000 people travelled to Bray on excursion trains.

In 1906 the company changed its title to the Dublin and South Eastern Railway. This was a successful company and the two lines from Bray to Dublin became the two busiest commuter lines in Ireland. However, the track between Killiney and Wicklow, due to its closeness to the sea, needed expensive and continuous maintenance. In October 1915 the line between Killiney and Bray was diverted further inland. At Bray Head a further diversion involved the boring of a 1,100-yard-long tunnel, the third longest in the country. Having completed these improvements, the company considered moving much of the Wicklow-Greystones section inland but the estimated cost was £250,000. This figure could not be justified during the First World War years.

The line suffered more than any other Irish railway from incidents during the 'Troubles', including the reduction to little more than scrap value of no less than 16 per cent of its first-line passenger locomotives by saboteurs. Such was the casualty rate that when two new main-line goods locomotives from Beyer Peacock arrived in Dublin in 1922 they were sent to Belfast for safe keeping until the Civil War was over. South of Bray, the railway service became sparse and slow even by Irish standards of the day. Six new passenger locomotives arrived from the London and North Western Railway and were named in honour of earls, amongst them the *Earl of Meath* and the *Earl of Wicklow*. They went into service on the Dublin–Bray passenger service but were not very successful. Five were sold to the British government and the one remaining (No. 64) was encased in armour plate and used to transport weaponry.

In the 1920s a team of scientists in University College, Dublin, headed by Dr James Drumm, developed a new type of low-resistance alkaline battery. In 1929 Dr Drumm patented the battery and following successful tests the Drumm battery train went into service on the Amiens (Connolly) Station to Bray line in February 1932. A further set came into service in August of the same year. Occasionally they were extended to Greystones.

The Drumm trains were introduced to the Harcourt Street–Bray line in 1939 when two more were brought into service. The Four Drumms, as they were affectionately known, provided almost the entire suburban service between Dublin and Bray during the coal shortages of the emergency years 1939–1945, apart from a period in 1944 when a government order prohibited the use of electricity for traction purposes. When the batteries were in need of renewal in 1949, seventeen years after the first train entered the service, the railway company decided against their replacement and removed the electrical equipment, using some of the carriages as steam-locomotive hauled stock. In the late 1950s the carriages were withdrawn and later scrapped.

In 1928 the Clayton railcar was introduced on the Bray line. They were similar to those of the London and North Eastern Railway, differing only in the size of the first class compartments. They cost £1,800 each and were fitted with a vertical boiler working at 300psi. They were withdrawn after three years and the coach sections converted to form three two-car articulated sets.

By 1939 there were fifty-three trains a day on the Dun Laoghaire line going as far as Dalkey, twenty of which went as far as Bray, while from Harcourt Street there were twenty trains serving stations to Bray. When Coras Iompair Éireann was implementing stringent economic measures in the late 1950s one of the most controversial decisions was the closure of the Harcourt Street–Bray line.

In 1984 the DART railway service – a fast and efficient link with Dublin and Howth – was introduced and was expected to do much in the development of Bray.

6

LOCAL GOVERNMENT

There is practically no information available on how Bray was governed for the period prior to 1850 as the Grand Jury Presentation Records were apparently destroyed. There is little evidence of public service of any significance being undertaken in the town. The vestry books of the Church of Ireland contained comprehensive accounts of funds being collected in the parish but almost all of those directly concerned church needs. Poor relief schemes were undertaken to ease the hardship of destitute families. Road overseers were appointed but there is no record of the work undertaken by them. In 1831 a local board of health was established. These are the only references to public works appearing in church records.

Between the 1851 and 1861 censuses the population of Bray increased by 23 per cent and in the following decade by a further 29 per cent. In the same period the number of dwellings rose by 62 per cent. This rapid development gave rise to some urgent basic requirements – sewerage, water, lighting and generally coping with the wide-ranging needs of an expanding town. In 1857 leading businessmen in the town decided to take advantage of the Towns Improvement Act (Ireland) 1854, which gave power to ratepayers to elect a body to govern their affairs. The town as defined for the purposes of self-government only covered the townland of Great Bray and the Lower Commons area. The first meeting of the commissioners was held on 9 November 1857. The commissioners present were P.W. Jackson, Joseph Bourke, Stephen Raverty, Thomas Miller, Edward Breslin, I.J. Waller, Henry Kingsmill, Andrew Kehoe, Thomas Darby, John Quin and Edmund O'Kelly. A decision was taken to elect the Earl of Meath as chairman of the board and it was agreed that commissioners would serve for periods from one to three years to maintain continuity.

When this effective local government was introduced the town was essentially a conventional county town which had acquired a superficial fashionable image through its houses and hotels. One of their largest projects was the enclosure of the commons of Bray for which an Act of Parliament was passed, the Bray Commons Enclosure Act 1859. On the land thereby acquired, a 15-acre People's Park was to be laid out, along with a 3-acre fair green and a road enclosing it. The park was laid out with orna-mental plants and shrubs donated by Lord and Lady Brabazon. Plots of land were sold in other parts of the commons for building and the money used to pay for the expensive improvements which were estimated to cost between £6,000 and £8,000. Of greater significance were the schemes for supplying the area with the basic services essential for a town rising rapidly in size and status.

Under the first committee gas lighting was introduced to the area. In 1856 the Bray Gas Company was formed, with Will Stears, an Englishman, as engineer. When the first stone of the works was laid in 1856 its capital was approximately £3,500. The gasworks were bordered by Bray Docks and on the south by Dock Terrace, the area now covered by the Harbour Bar and Scouts Den. The opening of the gasworks was regarded as such an auspicious occasion that a parchment manuscript describing the size, statis-tics, and government of the town was inserted in the foundation stone. When gas was piped to the town in 1860 the rate was 7s 6d per 1,000 cubic feet. Gas lamps were erected in prime locations, three on the Esplanade, four on Quinsboro Road, two on Seapoint Road and seventeen on the Main Street. The Bray Gas Company was too small to serve the entire area effectively and the supply was of poor quality. In 1864 the company was purchased by the Hibernian Gas Company and a new gasometer was trans-ferred from Kingstown to supply the area. £50,000 was spent on the project and the rate reduced to 6s 6d per 1,000 cubic feet. Despite the large gasometer the quality of gas remained weak and expensive.

Another important project initiated by the Commissioners was the town's sewerage network, in which sewers were laid in almost all the populated areas under its authority.

The total valuation of the town for 1857 was £3,551 15 0d although thereafter the figure rose considerably. When the question of Bray being constituted a township was first mooted at a meeting of the ratepayers in 1866, it was overwhelmingly rejected for fear that higher taxation would be introduced. As a result, the Township Bill, before it was submitted to Parliament, had a clause inserted fixing the maximum rate at 3s 6d (including water rates and sinking fund rate). The original commissioners governed the town for nine years until the area was constituted a township.

On 23 July 1866 the Act was introduced in Parliament for the Improvement of the Town and district of Bray in the Baronies of Rathdown, County Dublin and Wicklow. It stated:

The District of Bray is a large, populous and improving District, the population thereof has of late years greatly increased and is increasing; and whereas the Extension of the Limits of said Township and the Formation of the District into one Township, would be of local and public advantage.'

The boundaries of the township were given as follows:

The boundary commences at low-water mark on the sea shore at the north-eastern corner of the present township and thence along the centre of the boundary in the Bray River, thence westward along the centre of the said river to the boundary of the detached portion of the townland of Bray commons, thence southward along a stream through the townland of Killarney toll road leading to the old road from Bray to Newtownmountkennedy at the southern boundary of Killarney Cottage, thence in a south-easterly direction in a straight line to meet the stream in the townland of Oldcourt; thence southward along the said stream to a point where it is crossed by the Boghall Road to its junction with the eastern boundary of the townland of Killruddery Demense; thence northward and eastward along the said boundary to its junction with the road leading from Bray to Greystones; thence eastward along the boundary between the townlands of Newcourt and Ballynamuddagh to the sea; thence by the sea short to the point first named.

The township consisted of three wards to be named Little Bray Ward, East Ward and West Ward. The Little Bray Ward covered the area of the townships in County Dublin. The East Ward contained the portion of the township to the east of Bray Bridge and southwards along the centre of the Main Street and along the centre of the road leading to Greystones. The portion of the township to the west of this line was deemed to be the West Ward. The requirements for anyone standing for election as a commissioner under the Act were that he should be a resident within the township and that he should be rated for the Relief of the Poor at not less than £30 annually. A non-resident must own lands or tenements in the township to be rated at not less than £100.

The first commissioners were Edward Wingfield Verner, Matthew O'Reilly Dease and Alfred Sothern for Little Bray; John Quin, Charles Putland, Andrew Kehoe, Edward Breslin, Peter Warburton Jackson, Edmund William O'Kelly, John O'Neil, Stephen Lavery and James Thornton for the East Ward; and the Earl of Meath, George Hudson and William Dargan for the West Ward. The Earl of Meath was the first chairman and John Quin the deputy chairman. They held their meetings in the Old Courthouse. The emergence of names like Quin, Breslin, Dargan and Brennan on the lists of commissioners would suggest a determined progressive mood in the body as they were the most ambitious and enlightened promoters and developers in the town. These were men prepared to invest large amounts of money and would ultimately have most to gain from development. Breslin served as a commissioner for forty years until his death in 1897. Following Brennan's death in 1865, the International Hotel was represented by Charles Dufresne from 1870 to 1884. In 1880 he proposed the construction of an impressive sea wall. John Lacy, owner of the Bray Head Hotel, was a commissioner between 1883 and 1886.

Almost all the important landowners were represented at this stage but over the following years as they stepped down from office they were gradually replaced by traders. Within this group there were varying degrees of wealth and status from mill owners and local coal importers who were owners of valuable property, to grocers, victuallers, builders, ironmongers and car owners. In general they were energetic and hard-working commissioners with a genuine interest in the welfare of the community. Martin Langron, an ironmonger, was a dedicated chairman following Sir Henry Cochrane of Woodbrook who was regarded as having a conservative influence. These men were more reluctant than the hoteliers to levy heavy taxation. Doctors, bankers, solicitors and military men also appear in the list of commissioners at this time. There were also some businessmen and merchants from Dublin, amongst them Edward Lee, owner of a chain of drapery stores, although these tended to be excluded in the main because they did not have the required residency qualifications. These merchants showed an enthusiasm and pride in their adopted town.

The commissioners required greater powers, including control over the roads formerly held by the county Grant Juries. Along with the statutory services, the township commissioner inherited the problem of the inadequate gas supply. They succeeded in reducing the cost of gas to 5s 6d, but this was still a higher rate than in Kingstown or Dublin. In 1874 the commissioners opposed a bill in Parliament which threatened to raise the price of gas considerably, and as a result an agreement was reached whereby Bray was supplied with gas at the lower rate charged in Dalkey. The township commissioners increased the number of street lamps and there was a noticeable improvement in the service in the mid-1870s. As a result of the Alliance of Dublin Gas (Bray Supply) Act 1877, new mains and pipes were laid in the town for the extension of the supply. Complaints concerning the supply continued into the mid-1880s, when electric light was introduced to the Esplanade area during the summer months. The head-race situated in the old mill building beside the river turned the turbine of the electricity company but the commissioners were not impressed by the first installations of the new service. A provisional order was granted by the Board of Trade under the Electric Lighting Acts 1882 and 1886 to the commissioners to set up the Bray Electric Light Works in 1896. The town was not successfully lit by electricity until the early years of the twentieth century. The entire scheme cost the township £20,000.

The provision of running water to the area had been a constant problem. The first commissioners had made several attempts to supply a service but none had materialised. The absence of a reliable source of water gave rise to constant complaints. Edward Breslin was one of the strongest critics on the subject following the destruction of his stables by fire due to the lack of an effective water supply. In the 1866 Township Act provision was made for the supply of River Vartry water to the area by Dublin Corporation. Following the initial outlay of £4,000 for laying pipes, water was finally introduced in April 1869. To finance the supply a special Water Rate of 1s in the pound (about £600 per annum) was struck. The entire scheme was a major operation by the standards of the day, costing £600,000. The supply was weak because the corporation had underestimated the population. The Act had specified that twenty gallons of water per person per day were to be supplied. In 1874 the number of complaints encouraged the commissioners to erect a meter to check the quantity of water coming into the town. Subsequently the supply improved and the complaints decreased. The scheme provided many bridges where the mains were carried across the Dargle and Glencree rivers. Elegant valve towers and caretakers' cottages were another aspect of the scheme and they still exist along the Enniskerry Road and in the Dargle Valley.

The construction, improvement and maintenance of roads were other major undertakings by the commissioners. They opened a new road through the commons (Dargle Road) and took over many private roads that they paved, fenced and kept in good repair. With the exception of major projects, the work of repairing and constructing smaller roads and paths was carried out under annual contracts. The maintenance of the Esplanade was also the responsibility of the commissioners. This entailed keeping the railings along it in good repair, laying lawns and providing seating. Under the commissioners, by-laws were issued forbidding the landing of boats or nets on the strand, forbidding meeting there and requiring a decent standard of dress on the beach. There were regulations for the proper maintenance of beach boxes and for the segregation of male and female bathing boxes. In 1875 the commissioners took over the ladies' baths in the centre of the Esplanade from the Bray Pavilion Company.

The commissioners tackled the problem of laying sewers by borrowing £20,000 in March 1867 for the project. By 1870 the sewage system from the town, including the newly built areas, was almost completed. There had been many complaints about the lack of sewage before 1866 but with the improvements implemented, the problem was eradicated. It was necessary to provide outlets for sewers and to improve the dock because sewage was polluting the river that had previously been used as an outfall. These plans were completed in 1891 when outfall sewers for the entire area were enclosed in the two harbour breakwaters. The commissioners entrusted the maintenance of satisfactory sanitary conditions to medical officers and nuisance and sanitary inspectors.

In 1867, when the town was struck by a cholera epidemic, the worst effects were offset by the skilful handling of the problem. Judging from the large amount of work undertaken in 1866 in closing open drains, draining cesspools and clearing blockages, the town would appear to have been a serious health hazard prior to this date. Inadequate housing, including some primitive dwellings and old dilapidated buildings, which was considered to constitute health risks was demolished. Two years later the sanitary conditions had improved and the health and nuisance officers declared themselves satisfied.

The most important factor upon which all these ventures depended was finance. While the people were in favour of new amenities, not all were prepared to finance them. The minute book of the commissioners stated that a levy of 1s 8d for 'sanitary purposes' was authorised under the Sanitary Act. When a bill to levy extra rates for the harbour improvement was introduced it had an easy passage considering it was the most expensive and least profitable to date. The Township Act provided for borrowing on mortgage of the rates and it was with this method that the commissioners financed many schemes. The rate struck by the first commissioners remained static at 1s but it was obvious that no progress could be made under such limitations. On occasions shortage of finance forced the delay of projects until the next rate was collected. The rate rose rapidly in 1883 to 4s and in 1892 to 5s, but whenever possible the commissioners reduced the rates.

Many ratepayers considered the issuing of by-laws, of which there was quite a profusion in the early days of the township, to be extravagant and these were curtailed. By-laws were issued regulating lodging houses for which minimum standards of ventilation and sanitation were laid down. Post offices had to be licensed and there were by-laws forbidding the wasting of water and regulating charges by hackney drivers.

Township duties also involved the commissioners in an amount of legal work and, to deal with the large volume, a full-time solicitor was engaged. All legislation which might prove advantageous was investigated with a view to introducing it to the town. A noticeable trend was the increase of Catholic Commissioners. Of the first commissioners elected in 1857 under the Towns Improvement Act 66 per cent were Protestant but by 1880 the number was equally divided between the two denominations. Soon afterwards the Catholic commissioners outnumbered their Protestant colleagues.

7

THE BRIGHTON
OF IRELAND

The coming of the railway, combined with the Victorian belief in the beneficial effects of seawater, transformed Bray into a fashionable resort. A
degree of Anglicisation and pretentiousness is suggested by the adoption of
the sobriquet 'the Brighton of Ireland'.

Until the arrival of the railway many roads and avenues near the station
had not been named. The Main Street had improved over the years, with
two-storey houses gradually replacing cabins, but it still maintained its small
country town character. Access to the sea was difficult as the only public
route was the rough and stony Seapoint Road. The only other route was
through the private grounds of Quin's Hotel. The lands south of the hotel
to Bray Head were owned by the Putlands of Newcourt (Sans Souci, later
Loreto Convent) and Bray Head Demesne.

The positioning of the station at a point just south of the river changed
that existing pattern. John Quin, one of the first to realise the potential of
a prime connecting road between the town and the station as early as
October 1852, began transforming his path leading to the sea as a public
road. Building sites were sold on either side for terraces, villas and ornamental lawns. Simultaneously Quin refurbished the exterior of his own
hotel.

Part of these lands were purchased in 1854 by a friend of William
Dargan, Edward Breslin, who had been the caterer at Dargan's Industrial
Exhibition in Dublin and whom the railway company had placed in charge
of the Bray Railway Refreshment Rooms. Breslin purchased a site to the
east of the station and built a hotel which he named the Royal Marine
Hotel. Nearby he built an elevated terrace, consisting of a number of
exclusive villas and fitted them out with an elegant décor. Some years later
he bought all of John Quin's property, making himself one of the largest

landowners in the town. With the exception of Dargan, Breslin did more to advance the interests of the town and promote its growing prosperity than any other individual.

By the end of 1854 building sites for villas were being sold near Bray Head, advertised as being within two minutes' walk of the station. Thereafter many large and fashionable terraces were built along the seafront and adjoining roads including Fitzwilliam Terrace, Brennan's Terrace and Duncairn Terrace. Some of the most impressive buildings, Esplanade Terrace and Elsinore (now the Strand Hotel), were constructed by Sir William Wilde (father of Oscar).

In 1860 John Lacy opened the Bray Head Hotel. Swimming baths were erected at the northern end of the strand. The private avenue of Novara House (previously Bayview) stretching between the town and the sea was opened the same year, becoming a public road soon afterwards. In 1862 the International Hotel opened beside the station. The 180-bedroom hotel, which acquired this name because it coincided with the opening of the International Exhibition in London, was built by Sir John Brennan at a cost of £24,000 and was one of the largest hotels in Ireland. The *Handbook of Ireland* referred to it as 'an immense palatial pile and one of the finest buildings of its kind in the empire'. Initially it was not successful and was taken over by Breslin, under whose management it prospered. These hotels were patronised in the main by visitors from Ireland, England, France, Italy and Germany. That same year Charles Putland opened a road on his demesne running from Newcourt-Vevay to the strand, and close to the sea erected a large terrace of elegant residences.

Almost every new road at the time was linked to the seafront with the exception of the one that Sir Sidney Herbert opened through his demesne to Enniskerry. This road (later named Herbert Road in his honour) followed the course of the river and many gracious houses sprang up along it almost immediately. The entrance to the town was greatly improved by the demolition of the old bridge, which was inadequate for the flow of traffic and considered dangerous. The present bridge was constructed in 1856 by David Edge.

The railway had provided the conditions for the growth of the town but it was the initiative of William Dargan that made the prospect a reality. He was not the first businessman to realise the potential nor the first to develop it, but he was the person who contributed most foresight and drive to the emerging resort. He was at the height of his prestige and popularity with the success of his railway projects; he organised and financed the ambitious Great Dublin Industrial Exhibition, which was held in the building erected for that purpose, now the National Gallery. Queen Victoria was so impressed when she visited the exhibition that she offered Dargan a baronetcy but he declined the offer.

Speaking at a dinner for the opening of the International Hotel, Dargan stated that Bray was 'unsurpassed for scenic beauty in the whole of the civilised world. The hand of nature has done much already and it now remains for man to beautify and improve it still further.' There was no limit to Dargan's generosity and the press of the day referred to him as 'the man with his hand in his pocket'.

In 1854 Dargan encouraged Breslin in his hotel enterprise. He realised that the town's most important asset at that time was the seafront and that its potential should be exploited to the full. His first independent scheme was to take a long lease on the ground running parallel with the shore and the houses then being rapidly built opposite, from the Earl of Meath. He was aware of the rugged nature of the seashore and realised that something more impressive and in keeping with a fashionable town would be essential if Bray were to attract visitors. He cleared stones and rubble, levelled the surface and planted seeds to convert the area into a landscaped promenade. At an additional cost of £300 he erected a vulcanised fence and laid a road running parallel with the length of the esplanade. It did not run as far as Bray Head as the intervening section was being used as a rubbish dump, but he finally obtained permission from those who had rights over the property and extended the esplanade to the Head. This undertaking, which was completed in 1859, cost him £400 which he paid himself. Later, band stands, flower beds, palm trees, seating and other decorative amenities were added.

In October 1860 William Dargan was elected to the township commissioners and on 24 June 1861 a special meeting was held by the commissioners with a view to taking over the esplanade. A draft lease of the esplanade from the Earl of Meath to the commissioners was submitted and approved. Dargan agreed to keep the property in repair during his lifetime and thereafter it was to become the responsibility of the commissioners.

He next turned his attention to the Quinsboro Road (once called the Forty Foot Road) where building had already commenced at the end nearest the town. He also constructed Ravenswell Road, on the north side of the river, and a bridge under the railway to provide a more convenient route to the seashore on the Dublin side. In 1857 Dargan drew up plans for the Turkish Baths which were built at a cost of £8,500 and opened to the public two years later. They were one of the first of their kind in Ireland, built in a Middle-Eastern style reminiscent of the Brighton Pavilion. Such an enterprise firmly established Bray as a fashionable resort, similar to the rising seaside towns on the English coast, of which Brighton was the most prestigious. To accommodate invalids frequenting the baths, a hydropathic institute was established nearly in Galtrim House managed by Dr Haughton, an advocate of the usefulness of the original bath. The official *Railway Handbook* said of the baths:

Hot air-moistened and fresh, but without visible vapour – consequence
perspiration, and the complete cleansing of the multitudinous pores of the
skin from within and not from without, forms the vital principle of the
bath.

The baths with separate areas for men and women were open daily from 6
a.m. to 11 p.m. The admission charges were: public baths 2s or twelve for
18s; private baths 3s or twelve for 27s, which included bathing dresses,
sheets and towels. Shampooing, if required, was 6d extra but was not
allowed on Sunday.

The valuation of the baths was £200 in 1861, on which a rate of £10
was payable. The management of the baths was entrusted to Dr Barter, who
had already established his name with his baths in Blarney, County Cork.

To the east of the Turkish Baths Dargan erected ten expensive residences
consisting of two blocks of semi-detached houses at either end and a
terrace of six houses in the centre. They were named after him, but in later
years, the name of the terrace was changed to Duncairn. He also planned
to build another terrace of a similar type but this project did not materialise. Between the baths and Quinsboro Road he laid out grass and trees
and a private avenue. To the east of the houses he established a games
ground where a wide range of sports and entertainment were performed.
The attendance at the first sports event in the grounds (later to be called
Carlisle Grounds) in September 1862 included the lord lieutenant and a
large number of distinguished guests. Many summer events were held
annually, including charity bazaars and agricultural and horticultural shows
for which the railway company donated the main prizes.

The natural and material impetus provided by Dargan and the railway,
along with the other progressive speculators, changed the appearance of
Bray from that of a fishing village to a seaside resort within the span of a
decade. In the second half of the nineteenth century residential Bray grew
rapidly. Between 1851 and 1871 the population rose from 4,151 to 6,504
and over the next two decades increased further to 7,422. As the town's
reputation grew, the nobility and gentry came to live there in large
numbers. Resident landlords included Lord Viscount Powerscourt, Lord
Viscount Monck, Earl of Meath, Sir George Hodson, Charles Putland, D.C.
La Touche, Alexander Boyle and Phineas Riall. The upper middle classes
began to find that Bray possessed a social status attractive to aristocrats,
wealthy gentlemen and professional people. Soon judges, barristers, high-
ranking army officers, doctors, professors, prominent artists, writers and
musicians and a large number of Dublin businessmen and traders (amongst
them reputable names like Switzer, Morgan and Guinness) found a haven
in Bray. Some were prominent residents, while others merely had their
summer homes in the town or surrounding countryside, paying up to

£150 a month for houses facing the sea. In addition to bringing prestige to the town, they also spent their income in useful improvement of buildings, planting trees and the general fertilisation of the soil from which they derived their rents.

By now Bray consisted of stately mansions, hotels, private residences, villas and public institutions built in well-laid-out streets and terraces, with front and back gardens. The town and district offered considerable educational advantages as there were several high-class private and elementary schools. A major attraction were the long leases being offered on properties in the developing area of the Strand, Quinsboro Road and Novara Road where leases of 900 and 999 years were quite common. This encouraged people to reside in Bray in preference to such areas as Kingstown where leases were much shorter.

The overall standard of housing in the area improved greatly from the mid-1850s. The new houses were both larger and architecturally superior to those previously constructed. The Strand Road that had been the preserve of fishermen (known locally as 'seagulls') and the poorer classes was by 1870 completely dominated by large and elegant terraces. Fishermen, in the main, moved to Dock Terrace and other poor families to houses in Little Bray. By now there were a number of fashionable terraces on Quinsboro Road, Duncairn (formerly Dargan) Terrace, Princes of Wales Terrace, Royal Marine Terrace and Goldsmith Terrace. Houses built by Mr Putland in Sydenham Road and the newly developed Meath Road tended to be smaller and varied from small terraced houses to large detached residences. The rate for a bed in a hotel for a single night was 2s 6d and 1s 8d for breakfast.

As early as 1860 many tourist guides and handbooks were referring to Bray as 'the Brighton of Ireland'. This comparison was both significant and beneficial: at this time not only was Brighton the most popular and respectable of English seaside resorts, but due to rail links it had become one of the most fashionable of London's residential satellites. Dargan and other developers had consciously set out to mould Bray into a fashionable area, using Brighton as a model.

In colourful prose J. Gaskin in his *Irish Varieties* gives the following description of Bray:

> The magnificent mile-long promenade was framed on one side by a shelving beach with a variety of rare and curious pebbles and shells. Opposite are beautiful and stately marine villas, well arranged terraces and mansion of noble proportions and architectural beauty, palatial hotels and oriental concert halls. These elegant and curiously embellished structures were originally designed for Turkish Baths where invalids and convalescents might not only face the breeze and catch its sweetness, but revel in the

luxury of an Eastern bath with all its anodyne accompaniments and restorative qualities, whilst sojourning in the pursuit of health, pleasure and relaxation in the capital refined and aristocratic of picturesque Wicklow, within an easy distance of the grand and wondrous scenery of this charming county.

Another guidebook of this period stated that 'when dark cloud and heavy rains may be seen in the direction of Dublin and Howth, the sun is shining brightly on Bray and the Head'. In his *Irish Sketch Book* William Makepeace Thackeray describes a journey from Kingstown and his first glimpse of Bray:

> A two-horse car, which will accommodate twelve, or will condescend to receive twenty passengers, starts from the railway station for Bray, running along the coast for the chief part of the journey, though you have but a few views of the sea, on account of intervening woods and hills. The whole of this country is covered with handsome villas and gardens and pleasure grounds.

Thackeray also described approaching Bray from the west.

> A long tract of wild country, with a park or two here and there, a police barracks perched on a hill, a half-starved-looking church stretched its long, scraggy steeple over a wide plain, mountains whose base is richly cultivated while their tops are purple and lonely, warm cottages and farms nestling at the foot of the hills, and humble cabins here and there on the wayside, accompany the car that jingles back over fifteen miles of ground through Enniskerry to Bray.

Following the interest of the first few years, the popularity of the Turkish Baths diminished and in 1867 they were converted into Assembly Rooms which featured cultural evenings of song, concerts and drama. In December 1868 the Alexandra Masonic Lodge leased a wing of the building for use as a meeting place. Later it was converted into McDermott's Picture House and sadly it was recently demolished to make way for yet another shopping centre.

In 1876 a skating rink was erected on the strand which was reputedly one of the best in these islands and attracted many visitors. A pavilion to contain a marine aquarium, concert rooms, reading rooms, refreshment lounge and an exhibition hall with grounds laid out with a skating rink, croquet lawn and archery grounds were planned but never came to fruition. Several attempts were made to construct a Brighton-type pier in Bray but in each instance they fell through. Dargan did lay out a less ambitious recreation ground where cricket, archery, croquet, polo and rifle clubs operated and sports events were held. On a terrace facing the ground a fashionable men's club with reading rooms was established.

The people of Bray were sad on learning of the death in Dublin of William Dargan, aged sixty-two. His life had been spent on improving the lot of his fellow man. He had never fully recovered from a fall from a horse the previous year and his inability to attend to his affairs brought acute financial difficulties. In Dublin a statue of Dargan was erected during his lifetime in Merrion Square in front of the National Gallery. In Bray, to which he devoted so much of his time, fortune and talents, a street and a bridge bear his name.

In 1875 the Bray Amusements committee was formed, consisting of prominent residents and businessmen, and, funded by subscriptions from local inhabitants and the railway company, they organised entertainment for locals and visitors. During the summer season they spent an average of £765 arranging for military bands to play weekly on the bandstand with the railway transporting the bands free of charge and providing the use of the covered station platform during inclement weather. These bands included the Sixth Reserve Cavalry Regiment and the Third Battalion Royal Irish Rifles. They also arranged polo matches, swimming galas, rowing regattas, races, athletic meetings, steeplechases, firework displays, flower and dog shows and balloon ascents. The majority of these events were held in the Carlisle Grounds, which Edward Breslin offered free of charge on these occasions. An entrance fee ranging from 1s to 2s to the grounds was introduced to exclude the large number of working-class people who were attracted to open-air events held on the esplanade. It was felt that their unruly manners would inconvenience the upper classes. Reasonable reductions were offered to those holding return railway tickets. It was believed that even the third class and excursion fares were beyond the reach of the poorer classes.

There was a wide range of shopping facilities, with many shops providing the basic necessities while others reflected the more exotic taste of the new up-market residents. There was a hairdresser and perfumery who boasted the patronage of the Prince of Wales, cigar and tobacco merchants, wine and spirit merchants, silk dealers and milliners. Almost all of these ships were situated on Quinsboro Road.

The 'Brighton of Ireland' aura did not, however, cover the whole town. Little Bray, which formed a sort of Irish town outside the English-style area, was definitely not part of it. Here housing consisted mainly of the thatched cabins and the population was almost entirely working class, where the influence, sophistication and mannerisms of the more prosperous areas had little relevance.

Besides the more mundane duties of running an expanding town, the Town Commissioners acted as a most effective tourist board. They maintained high standards in hotels, lodging houses and bathing boxes, set in place controls against overcharging and dishonesty amongst those dealing with the public, and took action against any activities which threatened to blemish the reputation of the town. An example of this determination was the strenuous measures taken to curb the unethical conduct and dishonesty of the local hackney drivers, some of whom had bad reputations. The commissioners also published the main guidebooks to the town and in these constantly highlighted the virtues of Bray and its suitability for both holidays and residence. They were to the fore in destroying the town's old market and fishing reputation and strove to cultivate and maintain the new image.

One of the first set of by-laws issued by the commissioners provided for the transfer of markets and fairs, formerly held along the Main Street to the bridge, away from the fashionable areas to the commons in Little Bray. Similar measures were taken to ensure that the strand developed an exclusively tourist character. While constructive measures were taken to make the esplanade the preserve of tourists and visitors, fishermen continued in their centuries-old tradition of landing catches and bringing their nets onto the beach to dry. By-laws were issued forbidding such practices but, following complaints about the hardship caused, a compromise was reached. The fishermen were permitted to land their craft and dry their nets on a small stretch of beach opposite Claddagh Terrace, towards the northern end of the strand where they would least interfere with the strolling gentry.

The most successful and rewarding project undertaken by the commissioners was the sea-wall and promenade, completed in 1886. They undisputedly became one of the greatest tourist attractions in the town. The title 'Brighton of Ireland' was taken so seriously by the commissioners that in 1874 they sent for copies of the by-laws operating in Brighton for use as a guideline in drawing up the by-laws for Bray. Edward Breslin, chairman of the board, stated in a speech that money would have to be spent if Bray was to 'be what it should be – The Brighton of Ireland'. In a guidebook published by the commissioners in 1884 a comparison was made between Bray and Brighton in which the latter came off worse – 'We fearlessly assess that the natural advantage of Bray, derived from its position, proximity to the metropolis and the varied beauty of the surrounding scenery, confer on it a title to pre-eminence which Brighton or Scarborough or the much sought-after English watering places can never attain to.'

8

THE SEA

For many centuries the sea has been both a friend and an enemy of Bray. The annual tumultuous spring and autumn tides have been responsible for heavy flooding with loss of life, shipwrecks, damage to property and constant erosion of the beach and cliffs. Between 1860 and 1877 the sea flooded the new esplanade five times and it remained one of the greatest problems for the commissioners to overcome. On numerous occasions huge waves lashed the Esplanade, making large breaches in it, flooded the Strand Road, submerged the ground floors of Martello Terrace and threatened the houses along the Strand Road. Temporary preventative measures, such as piling with stones, were attempted as remedies but were to no avail. Annually the commissioners faced the costly task of repairing the damaged areas at either end, close to the mouth of the river and Bray Head. A fund was set up to address the problem and subscriptions to it were numerous and substantial. With the capital raised, a strong piling reinforced with larch beams was erected in the affected areas. The winter storms that year destroyed the piling as it had previous precautions, causing an estimated £200 worth of damage.

In 1873 storms and flooding badly damaged the gasworks and for several days the town was without lighting. In 1876 the Kingstown lifeboat rescued the crews of two ships, the *Vesper* on the Kish Bank and the *Leonie* off the coast of Bray. On the return trip with the rescued men the lifeboat itself capsized and four were drowned.

By 1877 man's battle with the sea had reached crisis proportions, with storms at the beginning of the year flooding fishermen's cottages near Bray Head to a depth of 4ft. Cabins were washed away, fishing boats destroyed and parts of the railway line around Bray Head were washed away. The situation created what the *Freeman's Journal* described as 'the most fearful scene of disaster and destruction'. It was obvious that if the flooding continued the fashionable seaside areas would soon be evacuated and the town's image diminished.

In February 1879 a paper was read to the Institute of Civil Engineers of Ireland by G.H. Kinahan which identified the cause of the flooding as erosion of the beach. This process, initially gradual, had been radically accelerated by the building of a dock by the railway company in 1858. Previously the river had entered the sea sluggishly through many natural channels and had not seriously affected the drift of sand southwards to the beach. The problem became acute when one channel was formed and made permanent by the construction of strong river walls, situated close together to narrow the river and increase its depth and flow and prevent silting by carrying the sand out to sea.

By 1880 the commissioners, realising the serious consequences this coastal erosion would have on the area, especially the strand, began to consider emergency measures. At a meeting of the town commissioners on 1 March 1887 Charles Dufrense of the International Hotel put forward a suggestion of a concrete sea wall to protect the strand against the encroachments of the sea. The original plan was to build a simple protective wall with a parapet running the length of the beach with a gravelled promenade inside it for an estimated £2,500. The plan was improved when the commissioners realised that what had begun as an emergency engineering scheme might, with additional capital, be transformed into a valuable asset to the area. To undertake the enormous task, the engineer P.F. Comber was requested to draw up plans.

The plans provided for an 18ft-high sea-wall, 1,043 yards long, with an embankment reinforcing it. It was designed so that the top of the sea wall and embankment would be 3ft above the original esplanade level, acting as a storm barrier for the esplanade. The sea wall constructed of Portland cement with granite copings was built at the high water mark with a curved sea-face in order to send the waves back out. Nine-inch drainage pipes were built into the structure to drain the esplanade. Ornamental metal railings were placed on top, to run the length of the sea wall except where six sets of steps led down to the beach. The embankment was designed to act as an 18ft wide promenade that would be asphalted and would slope gradually towards the sea for drainage. Behind this embankment, on the part nearest the esplanade, a low wall was to be built to further protect the area. This wall was to serve as a seat and would be finished with an ornamental back. This seating would continue along the length of the promenade except in the seven places where steps only, and four places where steps and ramps for invalid chairs, were to be erected with ornamental gas lamps at either side.

The plans were enthusiastically received by the commissioners and following a submission to Parliament an Act was passed in 1881 authorising the building of the sea wall and promenade. Lord Brabazon had been largely responsible for its quick passage through the House of Commons. In May 1884 tenders for the scheme were advertised and one from McAlpines of Glasgow for 441 yards, at a cost of £5 per linear foot, was accepted. Although the contract went to a Scottish contractor, the project gave work to many unemployed local men affected by a general economic depression at the time. The first section, finished in August 1885, was opened at an impressive ceremony in September by the Lord Lieutenant, Lord Carnarvon. Electric lighting was installed on the Esplanade the same year. In May 1885 the second section was tendered for, and once again McAlpine's tender was accepted. The section was 602 yards long and the cost reduced to £14 15s 6d a yard. This section was officially opened in August 1886. In 1890, when the Harbour Act was passed, provision was made for the extension of the sea wall further south towards the Head. The total cost of the project was £20,000 for the two sections completed in 1886 and a further £5,000 for the later section. An Act of Parliament authorised the issuing of debenture stock to finance the work. Township bonds were launched, issued at £100 each. Under the Harbour Act a clause was inserted authorising the commissioner to consolidate their debts. Existing debts were paid off with a large loan from the loan commissioners, repayable over sixty years at 3½ per cent to relieve taxation, and the issue of debenture stock was authorised.

During the winter after the completion of the first sections, six cracks appeared in the ashphalted promenade during heavy storms. In 1887, five more cracks appeared. They were repaired and in the following years further damage was detected. The Grand Marine Promenade, as it became known, provided the necessary seating for the esplanade, facilitated walks by the sea and the movement of invalids, and a new sophisticated dimension was added to Bray's tourist appeal. It vastly improved the appearance of the sea front area and constituted the most publicised feature of the area.

In the early years of the nineteenth century an attempt had been made by Mr A. Nimmo to construct a harbour at Bray. Nimmo's was the first of many abortive endeavours over the next eighty years. There were many reasons why a harbour was necessary for the town. Firstly there was a large fishing fleet which, due to the absence of a harbour or a dock, was forced to land its catches and boats on the beach, where the vessels were frequently damaged by storms. Secondly, there was a lucrative import business. For nearly a century Welsh colliers delivered coal weekly to Bray merchants and the gas works. 15,000 tons of coal were imported in 1880 and 20,000 tons of limestone passed through the port annually. There was also a passage of slate and a moderate export trade of timber and grain. The small vessels carrying these commodities had great difficulty in navigating the river to secure a landing place below the bridge on Seapoint Road, mainly as a result of heavy silting. Some schooners and ships called flats were discharged on the beach and could only be worked at low water by horses and carts loading at the ship's side. This work could only be carried out in good weather and was dangerous to ships in any weather; freight charges were consequently high. Thirdly, a harbour would be an advantage to Bray's tourist industry as it would facilitate the docking of many pleasure steamers which were active on the east coast.

The problem was further aggravated in 1853 when the railway company built a low bridge over the mouth of the river, blocking off the entrance to the berthing dock on Seapoint Road. Acceding to complaints, the Admiralty set up a commission to report on the situation. Their findings were that the Bray River was a navigable waterway only as far as the bridge. Consequently the railway company was ordered to provide a compensatory dock for the traders of Bray on the southern side of the river mouth outside the bridge. This dock was constructed in 1858 and was an improvement on the existing docking arrangements but was still susceptible to winter storms. It proved conclusively that a specially designed and constructed harbour was a necessity.

In the intervening years the matter was frequently discussed at the township commission meetings. Those advocating the construction of a harbour argued that such a facility would also be a source of revenue for the town. It was estimated that £360 could be collected annually in tolls. In 1861 Mr Matthew O'Reilly Dease offered £10,000 towards the building of a harbour at the mouth of the river, provided that the balance was put up by other benefactors in the town. Unfortunately this idea did not bear fruit.

Responding to mounting pressure, the commissioners began to investigate the feasibility of providing a harbour. In 1861 they commissioned a survey of the area and the resulting estimate costed the project at about £10,000. The commissioners felt confident that they could borrow this sum. In 1864 a bill was submitted to Parliament and an Act was passed for the improvement of the harbour. By September 1866 tenders for the preliminary work of cutting through the river mouth and piling were sought. In December an application was made by the commissioners to the Board of Trade requesting a loan for the scheme under the Fisheries Act. Early the following year a fund-raising committee for the harbour was set up and included such prominent residents as the Earl of Meath, Matthew O'Reilly Dease of Ravenswell and Edward Wingfield Verner of Corke Abbey. In May 1867 the Earl of Meath requested Mr Cotton, an engineer, to draw up plans for a harbour, costing not more than £10,000. The tender of Mr Newton Williams for completion of the preliminary work at £672 was accepted and work commenced in July. The Earl of Meath and

Wingfield Verner both recommended the project to the Board of Trade but in August 1861 their application was rejected.

Meanwhile, the first section of the preliminary work had been completed. The second portion ran into severe difficulties when bad weather delayed work and a section of the piling collapsed, damaging vessels in the dock and trapping them within it. With no funds to expand the project, the commissioners were forced to content themselves with completing the work of piling according to the contract and abandoned their hopes for a harbour. That winter the work completed was totally destroyed by the storms.

Despite frequent agitation by advocates of the scheme over the next decade, nothing was actually undertaken. The dock fell into disrepair and became unusable. The fishermen still experienced great difficulties with constant damage to their vessels. In 1880 a grant of £3,000 was made to Greystones, which immediately raised hopes that Bray would be the recipient of similar help. There was a general consensus that a major project would have to be undertaken to provide work for the huge number of unemployed in the area resulting from the nationwide distress at the time. Responding to pressure, the commissioners decided on 22 January 1880 to request Parliament to implement the Act to improve the harbour and offer financial assistance.

In due course a bill was submitted to Parliament and duly passed. In April the Commissioners of Fisheries met to consider the benefits to be derived from the bill and whether to make a grant. The following month their reply was announced. Despite pleas from many quarters, including the unemployed, they would concede to a grant for the harbour as Bray was not deemed sufficiently distressed and was not listed in the *Gazette* as a needy cause. For a number of years all emphasis was placed on the sea wall project and the harbour was temporarily abandoned.

In 1886 when the sea wall was eventually complete, the unemployed again mentioned the idea of a harbour. At the request of the commissioners, plans were drawn up by engineers P.F. Comber and G.C. Macassey. In 1888 a further application was made to Parliament for an Act to construct a harbour. On this occasion a grant was not sought and the commissioners decided to borrow the necessary finance. The move was approved at a meeting of the rate-payers. The Bill was eventually passed by the House of Commons in 1890 and in November the Hibernian Bank agreed to grant a loan for the £30,000 required for the scheme at an annual interest rate of 3½ per cent.

In accordance with the provisions of the Bray Township Act of 1890, the commissioners entered into a contract on 23 April 1891 with Messrs W.J. Doherty, Civil Engineers, for the construction of a small tidal harbour at the mouth of Bray River embracing an area between the north and south piers of about seven acres. To the north a pier was to be constructed beginning at the railway embankment and running in an easterly direction for 300ft to the high water mark, and from the high to low water mark for 300ft. From there it ran in a south-easterly direction for 270ft, making a total of 910ft for the entire northern breakwater. The southern pier, which would be more exposed to the strong tides and gales, was to begin at the southern end of the baths on the esplanade and extend in a north-easterly direction for 180ft to the low water mark. From there it would continue in the same line for 410ft into deep water, from which point it would be canted slightly to the north and carried 230ft, an overall length for the southern breakwater of 830ft. The opening for the harbour would be 90ft wide, and the plans provided for the accommodation of vessels of 8ft draught at low tide and 20ft at high tide. At the end of the southern pier a lighthouse with a revolving beam was erected in 1901. It was destroyed in a storm in September 1957. The northern pier, into which the sewer outfall pipes were built, had an outside wall built of granite and an inside wall of concrete. The southern pier was constructed of solid concrete with granite on its seaward face. The outer wall was built high enough to withstand heavy waves.

The scheme was completed on 10 August 1897 in less than four years. The original estimate of £30,000 was inadequate and an additional £14,000 had to be borrowed to complete the job. Additional work was carried out on the project over the next six years, including increasing the size of the north pier, dredging the entrance to the harbour and along the north pier giving accommodation to vessels drawing up to 12ft of water. Stores were built on the north pier, and the ground level raised next to the north pier for the storage of timber for export. A 3-ton steam travelling crane was also installed.

Bray was at last provided with a harbour that could contribute considerably to its prosperity. Lloyds listed it as a safe port and no ships were ever damaged or delayed except as a result of bad weather. The income from tolls, duties and rates from 31 December 1896 (when the Board of Trade approved a levy of 70 per cent of the full duties to be undertaken) to 31 March 1901 amounted to £1,298 13s 3d. A special harbour rate was levied on the district to meet the interest and a sinking fund, and amounted on 31 March 1901 to £1,539 8s 2d. The harbour, in addition to the sea wall and promenade, greatly enhanced the appearance of sea frontage. Two breakwaters were constructed to enable locals and visitors to continue their walks along the promenade and out along the piers. The new facilities also proved an asset to the fishermen. The one disappointing factor was that the tolls brought in insufficient finance to cover the frequent costly repairs and harbour dredging.

1 *The eastern side of Bray Head showing the Cambrian rock and tunnels, c.1907.*

2 *One of the valve towers in the Dargle Valley.*

3 *The Scalp and Sugarloaf Mountain, c.1900.*

4 Above *Bray Station with waiting sidecars, c.1890.*
5 Right *The twelfth Earl of Meath, c.1885.*

6 *The heads of estate departments at Killruddery House, c.1922.*

7 Opposite above *Painting of Powerscourt House by George Barret, c.1760.*

8 Opposite below *Jubilee Hall, Old Conna, now Elian's Spanish School, in 1992. On one occasion Daniel O'Connell was a guest here.*

9 *Conductor Christy Healy and John Byrne beside their single decker No.45 bus, c.1947.*

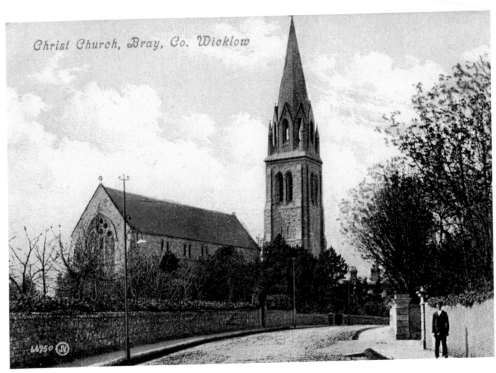

10 *The Church of Ireland Christ Church, c.1908.*

11 Above *A scene from the popular RTE television series Glenroe, c.1998. From left Alan Stanford, David Kelly and Nigel Mercier.*

12 Right *Garrett Flynn filming* The Old Curiosity Shop *at Ardmore Studios, c.1995.*

13 *Laurence Harvey filming a scene for* Of Human Bondage *at Seapoint Road, c.1965.*

14 *A view of Bray sea front on a summer's day, c.1996.*

15 *Hardy people enjoying the New Year's Day Charity Swim on Bray seafront, 1 January 2004.*

16 *Stormy day on Bray promenade, c.1996.*

17 *The mullet swans at Bray Harbour, 2001.*

18 *Aerial view of Bray, c.1950.*

19 *Royal Irish Constabulary, Bray Barracks, c.1916.*

At the peak of the harbour's activity in 1916, four shipments of coal were landed weekly and cargoes of pitch wood were exported. There were four coal merchants and three timber merchants using the port and it gave employment to about fifty dockers. They had a good reputation, as almost all ships using it could be discharged in one day, and as a result freights were standard. The harbour was also popular with pleasure boats, but it was impossible to keep it clean owing to the main sewer emptying into the harbour.

Bray Head

Immediately opposite the main gate of Killruddery estate is the entrance to a carriageway leading to the summit of Bray Head. Lined by mountain pines, it takes a circular route to render the ascent easier for horses. In the 1850s admission could be gained by signing one's name at the gate lodge and, if accompanied by a bicycle, paying a toll of 3d. Later a visitor who came by a vehicle could obtain a key for the upper gate at the lodge.

Bray Head, cloaked in heather and consisting of wooded slopes and rugged, forbidding cliffs, stands at 653ft above sea level and the highest point of the range is the Ordnance Flagstaff at 791ft. Sir James Ware, in his *Antiquities of Ireland* published in 1639, stated: 'Bray Head is a high and large cape; stretching a considerable way into the sea, on the south side of the bay of Dublin, from which a river and town take their names.' The head has always been a place of geological interest where rare plant species and wildlife abound. Some of the oldest fossils in the county are to be found in the Cambrian rocks there. From the summit one has a commanding view of the whole of Bray, the coastline across Dublin Bay, the Kippure mountains, the forests of Powerscourt, the Sugarloafs and, with good visibility, the Welsh mountains. A high wall, commencing at the seaside, ran east and west across the whole headland, dividing the property of the Earl of Meath on the south side from that of Mr Putland.

One of the most conspicuous features of Bray Head is the 30ft cross erected there in 1950 to commemorate the Holy Year. Constructed from mass concrete, the cross was blessed by Canon Moriarty, the parish priest, on 23 September that year, with 5,000 people in attendance. The inscription on its base reads '*Christo Regi* A.D. 1950'. The cost of the erection was met mainly by the children of the parish.

The Cliff Walk, originally named the Railway Walk, ran parallel to the railway line to Greystones. It was the property of the railway company as far as the gates of the Half-Way House. The remainder of the path southwards was on the property of the Earl of Meath, who allowed free passage every day except Friday. Close to this area was his own private beach reached by a concealed path. Dogs were forbidden past this gate. In 1861 the company made an agreement with the Earl for the provision of a

wooden footbridge from the Earl's road to the beach. In 1885 it was
replaced by an iron bridge and in 1895 it was removed as being unneces-
sary. Mid-way along the cliff is the look-out post on Cable Rock which
was used by the Coast Watching Service during the Emergency of
1939–45. Directly beneath the start of the walk is Naylor's Cove, later called
Bray Cove Baths. It was a popular swimming place and in 1906 the
Railway Company built a special platform beside the stone bridge to
service the cove.

Chair-lifts operated from the base of Bray Head for about twenty years
from the mid-1950s. The Eagle's Nest, the terminus for the chair-lifts, was
a popular centre for ballroom dancing in the 1930s and 1940s. It can also
be approached by the forty-seven steps near Raheen-an-Chluig – Little
Church of the Bell. The ruins of this church, sometimes known as St
Brendan's, still remain on the northern slope of the Head. The church is a
small rectangular building, erected in the thirteenth century, with the
remains of a door in the south wall and round-headed windows in the east
and west gables. An obelisk that was erected on Bray Head by W.P. Morris,
a Justice of the Peace, to commemorate the Jubilee of Queen Victoria in
1887, was blown up in the summer of 1933. Nobody was ever charged
with the offence.

9

THE BRABAZONS,
EARLS OF MEATH

For almost four and a half centuries the Brabazons have been one of the
most powerful and influential families in Bray. They have resided in the
stately Killruddery House, a mile south of Bray on the Greystones Road
since the mid-sixteenth century. The name Killruddery means Church of
the Knight and from ecclesiastical records it would appear that Killruddery
and Kilcroney were once subsidiary to the Prebend of Stagonil
(Enniskerry). In 1545 Sir William Brabazon received a grant from Henry
VIII of the monastery of Saint Thomas in Dublin. A section of the property
consisted of the lands of Kilrotheric (Killruddery) comprising the Little
Sugarloaf, Bray Head and the valley in between, where, some centuries
before, the monks had built a large rural retreat to which was attached a
chapel and burial ground. Lord Brabazon was granted the patent of
Killruddery at the yearly rent of £8 6s 8d along with two foot-soldiers for
the defence of the property. The entrance gate bears the family motto *Vota
Vita Mea* (My life is devoted).

The Brabazon family takes its name from the province of Brabant in
Belgium. Jacques le Brabazon accompanied William the Conqueror into
England as his standard-bearer in the eleventh century. The Irish connection with the family began when Sir William Brabazon was appointed
Vice-Treasurer and General Receiver in Ireland in 1536. He died in 1552
at Carrickfergus while in the north trying to subdue Hugh O'Neill and
the Scots. His eldest son, a Privy Councillor to Elizabeth I, was a Member
of Parliament for Wicklow and was created Baron of Ardee in 1618. His
son William was created first Earl of Meath in 1627.

William was succeeded by his son Edward, who had Killruddery rebuilt
in 1651, six years after it had been destroyed in the Civil War. In 1666 he
signed a partition agreement by which he added to his lands the section of
Great Bray between the Main Street and the sea and between the river and

the Main Street roughly to the north and west of the poundhouse. Edward was drowned in 1667 whilst on his way to London. He was succeeded by his eldest son, the third earl. He in turn was succeeded by his brother Edward, the fourth earl, who was appointed gamekeeper for all the royal parks in Ireland and fought with William III at Carrickfergus and the Boyne. He was wounded at the siege of Limerick. Edward married twice but died without an heir and, in 1708 another brother became the fifth earl. His eldest son, Chaworth, who succeeded him in 1715, married his aunt's chambermaid at a young age but they never lived together. After her death he married again, but there was no heir and his brother Edward succeeded to the title in 1758. Edward's son Anthony was MP for Dublin, and when he succeeded his father in 1772, the Corporation voted him the thanks of the city and a sum not exceeding twenty guineas enclosed in a gold box.

Anthony was followed by his son Willliam as ninth earl. At this time many of the gentry, including the Meaths, had their own militia. Tension arose when a member of the militia of Captain Gore of Kilpedder signed on with the earl. Captain Gore accused him of conduct unbecoming to a gentleman and challenged him to a duel that took place at Monastery near the Scalp in 1797. Lord Meath was wounded and died later of his wounds. The Meath family were outraged and claimed that Gore had fired too early. They charged Gore, who was defended by John Philpott Curran (father of Sarah Curran), but the case was dismissed. William, who was unmarried, was succeeded by his brother John Chambre as tenth earl. He was a Knight of Saint Patrick and Lord Lieutenant of County Wicklow. He was the last of the family to use the town house at 56 Saint Stephen's Green; he sold it to Mary Aikenhead for development into Saint Vincent's Hospital. On his death in 1851, he was succeeded as earl by William, who had been MP for Dublin from 1837 and was an honorary colonel of the Fifth Battalion of the Royal Dublin Fusiliers.

As Lord Brabazon, he presented a petition from Bray in favour of repeal to the House of Commons and was attacked by his Liberal colleagues for not instructing his tenants to vote Liberal during the elections. He constantly assisted the poor and in 1818 took over the barracks, which were seldom used following the 1798 Rebellion, and donated it to the three parishes of Bray, Old Connaught and Rathmichael for use as a dispensary and fever hospital. A grant towards the project was received from the Committee for the Suppression of Vice and from individual subscriptions. In the days of rampant typhus and cholera, there was urgent need for such a centre.

The twelfth Lord Meath was one of the promoters of the new fashionable image for the town and was the benevolent landlord of the greater part of the township. He undertook many capital works at no cost to the ratepayers. He was a natural choice as first chairman of the township commissioners, a post which he held with one short break until 1875 when he was forced to retire due to business commitments.

One of the most renowned hunts of all time was the Killruddery Hunt. At the time there was enough pasture to enable the hunters to chase the fox or stag from Bray Common to Kilternan, Carrickmines, Shankill, Dalkey, Glenageary, Monkstown and back to Dalkey. The hunters traditionally stopped at a popular inn opposite the gate of Loughlinstown House, run by a sporting gentleman named Owen Bray who was renowned for his exploits on his blind horse. Following the hunt, the riders partook of the hospitality of the Earl of Meath.

Between 1850 and 1870 there was a degree of political tension within the town and in particular a radical element amongst the commissioners. An arms survey of Bray a year before the Fenian Rising of 1867 produced only one ancient pistol and a gun and a small quantity of ammunition. There was speculation that the people of the town would be armed and reinforcements were brought in by the constabulary. This was intended to protect the town from a feared attack from without rather than within. Lord Brabazon recalled the period in his diary:

> On this occasion about a thousand Fenians marched on our town of Bray, where they expected to be joined by about an equal number of local sympathisers. My father, who was Lord Lieutenant of the county of Wicklow, on hearing the news, rode off to Bray to organise the police and to purchase ammunition. In the meanwhile his neighbour, Viscount Powerscourt, had ridden over to Killruddery to warn him. Finding him absent, Lord Powerscourt asked for my mother, who was in the garden directing the laying of some new flower-beds by the head gardener. Seeing Lord Powerscourt approach in haste, she became alarmed, and asked him what was the matter and whether anything serious had happened, especially to my father. On being told that the Fenians had risen she said something like 'Thank God – is that all,' and she then turned to continue her conversation with her gardener. She, like everyone else, had heard so much about the expected Rising for the past year that she had become tired of the subject and had lost all interest in it.

Any radical actions were swiftly dealt with: for example, a painter was arrested in November 1867 for responding to a toast to the Queen with the words 'To hell with the Queen.' In 1872 a large working-class crowd burned an effigy of Judge Keogh, who had sentenced many Fenian prisoners. Their conduct was never violent; it was more in the form of gestures of contempt. The working classes never belonged to the 'Brighton of Ireland' in either a spiritual or physical sense, and many bitterly resented the fact. However, not all the townspeople were pro-Fenian, as is evident from another entry in Lord Brabazon's diary:

> In the meanwhile the Roman Catholic labourers at Killruddery had met and had passed a resolution that they would offer their services to my father to defend the house. In Ireland, unfortunately religion and politics almost always go together, and therefore their resolution was more satisfactory.

In 1880, Lord Brabazon offered to build a new Market House and Town Hall for the town. The building that is situated at the top of the Main Street at the junction of Killarney Road and Vevay Road was designed by Thomas Newenham Deane and Son. It is an important example of the quaint Tudor-style architecture popularised in England by R. Norman Shaw and W.E. Nesfield in the 1870s. The main façade, facing down the Main Street, has tall narrow proportions, the side elevations being elongated. It consists of three bays and two storeys, built of red brick with a central carriage arch containing elaborate wrought-iron work. The ground floor served as a covered market. On the first floor was the Chamber Room, which was emphasised by three large oriels, transom and mullioned windows, each incorporating a large arch (known as Ipswich windows) with inserted coats-of-arms of the Brabazon family. A plaque at the entrance states 'This Town Hall and Market House was erected by Reginald Lord Brabazon, son of William 11th Earl of Meath and by Mary Lady Brabazon only daughter of Thomas 11th Earl of Lauderdale in the year of Our Lord 1881.'

Standing in front of the Town Hall is a unique stone fountain with a statue of a wyvern on top, which has been frequently mistaken for a devil by locals. The wyvern is a mythological creature whose upper half is a dragon and whose lower half is a serpent or viper. The wyvern comes from the Meath coat-of-arms and in the windows of the Council Chamber, wyverns can be seen in their correct armorial colours of gold with red wings and limbs, collared and chained in gold. Water troughs were erected at several junctures around the fountain.

A branch of the Land League, naming itself the Michael Davitt Branch, was formed in Bray in October 1881. From the outset it attracted large numbers of locals and reacted promptly to political events – condemning the arrest of Parnell and congratulating the election of a Home Rule candidate. In December 1883 a relatively minor event brought the under-lying tension to a head. Lord Brabazon began to discuss how the Town Hall could be utilised to best advantage. The commissioners requested the use of the proposed library in the Town Hall for religious, political and chari-table purposes but Lord Brabazon vehemently refused permission. He threatened to 'do no more' for the town if the commissioners persisted. Negotiations broke down and relations between Lord Brabazon and the commissioners were strained for a time. Finally Lord Brabazon reversed his decision, but not before the incident sparked off letters from 'Nationalistic Rate-payers' calling on the town to have nothing to do with the new Town Hall. In January the parish priest and a group of ratepayers stated that the Earl of Meath had a 'heart as Orange as Lord Rossmore'. That same month a large nationalist meeting was held in the town with the two main speakers William O'Brien and John Harrington, both MPs, expressing the hope that Bray would soon be emancipated from Killruddery. A meeting in the International Hotel, with fourteen ratepayers present, sympathised with the Earl of Meath for the attitude of the commissioners. This loyalist element, though a minority, never completely disappeared. Lord Brabazon wrote of this period:

> Off to Euston, where I met Reg [Brabazon] and was very pleased to get him back off stage again and saved from Ireland, where he had a dreadful time of it, what with Bray town commissioners to whom he wants to hand over the Market House, the Land Leaguers. They even threatened his life on Christmas Day. So much for gratitude amongst the poor easily led Irish.

The Town Hall was to become the meeting place for the town commissioners and was also utilised for a diverse number of social functions, dances and ceilis. The Irish Citizen Army had regular meetings there and in 1911 the Ancient Order of Hibernians began meeting there.

Following the 1894 election political allegiances began to shift: it was gradual at first but more rapid during the Land War at the end of century. Relations with Lord Meath, which had generally been harmonious, began to deteriorate as the working class began to demand their rights. Around this time one of the earliest trade disputes in the town broke out when labourers employed on the estate of Lord Meath went on strike for better conditions. As a result of poor organisation, the men were forced to capitulate and the strike was broken. Lord Meath demanded that the men seek forgiveness for their activities before they were reinstated. This gesture naturally hardened the men's attitude thereafter. At the time they were being paid 14s a week.

The generosity of the female members of the family was widely acknowledged and appreciated. The Dublin *Daily Express* of 14 December 1897 reported: 'The contribution of the Countess of Meath for the purpose of improving the conditions of workhouse girls in Ireland, is one of the most notable features in recent benevolence.' The Meaths were hosts to many prestigious international conferences including the Philanthropic Reform Association in 1901 at which the two principal subjects discussed were the Day Industrial Schools Bill and the proposed establishment of a home for comfort in Ireland for epileptics.

Reginald, the twelfth earl (1841–1929), was a colonel in the Royal Dublin Fusiliers, a Justice of the Peace for Wicklow, Deputy Lieutenant for County Dublin and Chancellor of the Royal University of Ireland. His son, the thirteenth earl, Reginald Le Normand (1869–1949), was in military service in the South African War and the First World War, reaching the rank of brigadier-general, having served with the Irish Guards and the Guards Brigade. The fourteenth earl, Anthony William Norman, born in 1910, was educated at Eton and served in the Second World War as a major in the Grenadier Guards and was wounded.

Many distinguished visitors were entertained at Killruddery. Not long after his coronation in July 1821, King George IV paid a visit to Bray with the Royal entourage receiving a tremendous welcome from the cheering crowds on route to Killruddery. The Earl of Meath built a new roadway the occasion through the Dargle Glen. Unfortunately the King never utilised it as his visit was curtailed.

In 1868 the Prince and Princess of Wales visited the demesne, when the Prince was stationed at the Curragh. The Lord Mayors of London and York were both visitors in 1875. William Gladstone visited Killruddery in 1877. He admired Christ Church but was critical of the absence of bells. He gave a donation of £50 to Lord Meath and encouraged the parish to make up the deficit. Lord and Lady Brabazon added £200 and in a short time, enough was raised to provide a peal of bells at a cost of £1,154. Another royal guest was the Queen of Romania in 1890; she was greeted by fireworks and a local band playing the Romanian national anthem. In 1897 the Duke and Duchess of York enjoyed the hospitality of Killruddery. Sir Walter Scott was greatly impressed with the demesne when he attended the open-air theatre. The Lord Lieutenants were frequent guests at functions and balls. Sir Robert and Lady Baden-Powell stayed overnight in Killruddery when they came to inspect respectively the Boy Scouts and the Girl Guides in Lord Iveagh's Park in Dublin. On 10 July 1911 the Prince of Wales and Princess Mary visited Lord and Lady Meath. The Prince planted a tree in the pleasure-grounds and inspected a guard of honour provided by the First Bray Troop of the Boy Scouts.

Killruddery House, the ancestral home of the Brabazons, is an imposing Elizabethan structure set in the secluded hollow between Bray Head and the Little Sugarloaf. The earliest painting of the building dates from 1680, when the Bray–Greystones road ran just east of the house. The exterior of the house is quite striking, with its pointed gables, bow window, armorial carvings, carved balustrades and surmounting cupola giving it an air of an old baronial seat. In 1820 the tenth earl had the present house greatly altered with a design by Richard and William Morrison, who were also responsible for Shelton Abbey, the home of the Earls of Wicklow. The original house had five bays and a hipped roof with a front door facing east.

In the middle of the twentieth century the size of the house, which was square with an inner courtyard, was reduced and the north and east wings demolished.

The interior presents a fine hall – wainscoted with oak and mellowed with the subdued light from stained glass and a fine reception room. The plaster work of the dining room ceiling is exceptionally decorative and much earlier in style than that in the drawing room. It was executed by a local man named Henry Popje from Bray in 1830. The dining room is part of the older building. A remarkable feature of the stair is the home-made wall clock with the face part of a dumb waiter, a bed warming pan for a pendulum and a bicycle chain to raise the weights. Of more importance are the historical portraits of the Brabazon family and many battle honours which adorn the walls. The library has Carolian-style decoration, alluding to the seventeenth-century origin of this section of the house. The bookcases are Chippendale, of eighteenth-century origin. There is a fine carved mantlepiece and overmantle after Grinling Gibbons, with a portrait of Charles II. The drawing room, originally hung with panels of silk, was designed by the Morrisons with the plasterwork by Simon Gilligan. His signature, dated 1824, is on top of the cornice. In 1852 a handsome conservatory and statue gallery was designed and built by William Burn in the fashion of the Crystal Palace in London, and it was filled with rare plants and life-size marble statues collected in Italy between 1830 and 1850. Of particular note is the one of Ganymede.

The magnificent residence is surrounded by extensive gardens, some over 300 years old. They are amongst the last surviving gardens of this period in Ireland. They are divided into three sections: the seventeenth-century gardens, the nineteenth-century gardens and the surrounding eighteenth-century park. Beside the steps leading from the forecourt is the granite balustrade, designed by Daniel Robertson, who was also the principal garden architect responsible for the garden layout at Powerscourt. On the left are nineteenth-century statues and box hedging. These statues and others of the same period in the garden were probably purchased at one of the Great Exhibitions held in Dublin in the middle of the nineteenth century to display work from continental factories. The path leads to a natural outcrop of rock that was developed as a rock garden.

Situated to the south of the main house are the seventeenth-century gardens comprising the Angles, the Long Ponds, the Sylvan Theatre and the Beech Hedge Pond. These gardens were designed and commenced when a French gardener, called Bonet, left Sir William Petty to work for the Earl of Meath in 1682. They were designed for the entertainment of a large number of people and their dimensions and layout is similar to that of a public park. A wall encloses each of the gardens. One of the strangest sights is the Sylvan Theatre cut out of the ground and surrounded by a bay hedge. Sir Walter Scott mentioned this theatre in his *Saint Ronan's Well*:

> At Killruddery, the seat of Lord Meath in the county of Wicklow, there is a situation for private theatrical exhibitions in the open air, planted out with evergreen which arise there in the most luxuriant magnificence. It has a wild and romantic effect, reminding one of the scene in which Bottom rehearsed his pageant, for a hawthorn break for a retiring room.

The Angles, sometimes known as 'The Monk's Walk' and said to date from the time of the monastery, form the middle section of the garden. Consisting of a series of walks flanked by hornbeam and beech hedging, they meet unexpectedly at various points in the centre. Beyond The Angles is an avenue of ilex trees and steps to a bowling green. The Long Ponds are twin canals 550ft long and known as *miroirs d'eau* – mirrors of water. Apart from the magnificent view they offer they are also stock with fish. Several Swiss lodges were constructed as gate lodges throughout the grounds. A memorial on the approach to Killruddery House about a hundred yards north of the Forecourt Gate bears the following inscription:

> *Underneath this stone do lie*
> *Bones of men of days gone by*
> *Those who in Christ's Faith have died*
> *Safe beneath His Cross abide.*

The inscription refers to bones discovered in the grounds and believed to be the site of a burial mound for the monks.

10

THE TROUBLES

In the early part of the twentieth century questions of political loyalty were hotly disputed and brought to the fore by the Home Rule League and other nationalistic groups, along with the loyalist group and the Bray Branch of the Irish Transport and General Workers' Union. Anti-imperialist sentiments were apparent on numerous occasions, such as in 1905, when Bray Urban District Council refused an address to King Edward to commemorate his coronation on account of the Oath. The proposal was defeated by seven votes to five. The trend of the working class towards socialism and the rousing of the nationalist spirit began to undermine the 'Irish Brighton' image and reports of their activities began to take precedence over the latter in newspaper coverage.

On 16 October 1905 the Saint Cronan's Branch of the Gaelic League leased a portion of the old disused mill at Church Lane for one year at a yearly rent of £7 10s. This is the first written record of the League's activities in Bray. They held Irish language and dancing classes twice a week and regular monthly meetings up to 1914. Concerts, *feiseanna* and sports events were organised regularly to pay the rent and teachers' fees. Amongst the prominent speakers who visited Bray were Dr Douglas Hyde and Patrick Pearse.

Despite strong moral and social support, there was little backing for armed resistance against British rule in the Bray area. A small company of Volunteers was formed in the town in November 1913 but they found it impossible to undertake any large-scale engagements. The company remained together for a year until the general split occurred and from the membership of 600 only a few remained loyal to the original Volunteer pledge. Immediately after the Howth gunrunning episode, a church gate collection for arms in Bray raised £30. Joseph Kenny, a member of the Irish Republican Brotherhood, passed the money to The O'Rahilly and in return received ten of the Howth rifles. Some of the Volunteers feared that the guns would be captured by the Royal Irish Constabulary, and nine of them were given to Liam Mellows.

With the outbreak of the First World War, recruitment meetings for the British Army were organised in the town and posters proclaiming 'Your Country Needs You' were prominently displayed. A number of local men were called up as British Army reservists and a large crowd gave them a rousing send-off as they left the station for active service abroad.

John Redmond, who was regarded as a Wicklow country gentleman at heart, together with John Dillon, were founder members of the Irish Nationalist Party whose main objective was Home Rule. Redmond and the Home Rulers ignored the Volunteers at first but on 20 September 1914, in a speech at Woodenbridge, County Wicklow, Redmond suddenly reversed his policy and called on the Volunteers not just to fight for Ireland but to go 'wherever the firing-line extends'. Redmond sought Lord Meath's official support and endorsement for the Volunteers but Meath saw it as a conflict of ideals. Redmond's enthusiasm overcame his initial reluctance and Meath asked Redmond for an assurance that 'by giving official support and encouragement to the nationalist Volunteers as His Majesty's Lieutenant for the county and city of Dublin I shall in no way fail in any loyal duty to His Majesty the King.' Meath decided to assist Redmond in his recruitment campaign and their co-operation was most successful. In September 1914 Lord Powerscourt addressed the Bray Volunteers and informed them that he had met Lord Kitchener and John Redmond regarding the recruitment of Volunteers. Joseph Kenny strongly objected and Lord Powerscourt left the meeting. Kenny was reported for interfering with recruitment for the British Army.

During the First World War Bray saw a considerable amount of military activity, with a training and firing range on Bray Head. Several premises in the town were occupied by troops, including the former Watkins Brewery. Frequent band recitals were given by military bands and they even staged a military musical fête. During the war the International Hotel was transformed into the Princess Patricia Hospital and several boys from Aravon School were given time off to assist the wounded soldiers. Teams of soldiers often played cricket against the school. Some soldiers in the hospital formed a group called the Blue Boys and organised concerts for other patients. Local people experienced great hardship during these years, caused by food shortages, and a section of the People's Park was set out in allotments to allow them to grow their own vegetables.

In January 1915 Desmond FitzGerald, a member of the Volunteers in Dingle, County Kerry, was ordered by the British authorities to leave the area within six days. He was forbidden to stay in Dublin and was informed that the area from Bray to within 20 miles of Arklow was open to him. He chose Bray and on enquiring if there was a company of Volunteers, Arthur Griffith gave him the name of a Sinn Féiner in the town who could introduce him to the Irish Republican Brotherhood. FitzGerald set about training the Volunteers in the Wicklow Mountains. Each Sunday the company had extended drill practice in the People's Park. In Bray he arranged a large meeting in favour of Home Rule at which The O'Rahilly was one of the main speakers. Soon afterwards FitzGerald ventured into Dublin by bicycle and was arrested for breaking the restrictions. He was tried in the courthouse, found guilty and sent to Mountjoy prison.

On Easter Sunday 1916 Arthur Griffith called at Joseph Kenny's home in Bray with instructions from Eoin MacNeill, cancelling all Volunteer activities that day. Griffith directed him to pass the message to the secretary of the local Volunteers, James McCarthy. Following confusion over the cancellation of orders, the Bray Volunteers played no part in the Rising other than cutting the telephone wires around the town. Desmond FitzGerald was released from Mountjoy on 31 March 1916 and joined the Rising in the GPO. He escaped capture and made his way back to Bray by way of the mountains but was arrested, court-martialled and sentenced to life imprisonment which was later commuted to twenty years. He was later released with the general body of prisoners.

In 1917 the Volunteers in Bray and Shankill were re-organised into C Company of the Third Battalion, Dublin Brigade. Weekly parades were held in Mitten's Field, Shankill, where members were trained in the use of guns and the making of improvised hand grenades. Night manoeuvres were organised around Puck's Castle, Ballycorus, and target practice was held in the nearby quarry.

In the 1918 General Election the company supported and helped secure the re-election of Sean Etchingham, a Sinn Féin candidate for East Wicklow. A Volunteer meeting was arranged at the Town Hall, and when the company attempted to march up the Main Street their path was blocked by a strong force of RIC men. Batons were drawn and confrontation was averted by the intervention of Father Michael O'Flanagan who advised the Volunteers to disperse. Later that year when Paddy Murphy, chairman of Sinn Féin Cumann, read the Proclamation he was arrested and jailed. The Volunteers were engaged in many minor operations such as the acquisition of record books from the home of an income tax inspector on Meath Road, and the seizure of minute books from the Town Hall. They copied a list of licensed firearm holders displayed in the post office but when raids were staged on the houses in the majority of cases the arms had been handed to the RIC for safe-keeping.

The volunteers had an arms dump at Shanganagh and a second one in a double tunnel on the railway line around Bray Head where they stored shotguns, cartridges and revolvers handed over by the Wicklow Volunteers at Newcastle. The arms were taken by Volunteers on a railway bogey to a dump and later transferred to an empty cottage at Shanganagh. There is an unconfirmed report that a consignment of arms was actually landed at Bray. The Dublin and South East Railway line was one of the most sabotaged lines in the country and some of its rolling stock was reduced to scrap. There was a sparse service south of Bray due to fear of attack. One engine was encased in armour plate and used to haul an armoured train.

In a raid on the Urban Council yard at the Fairgreen, crosscut saws, shovels and picks were taken and later used to dig trenches and block road in the area. The Volunteers, now ready for an all-out attack on the British, chose Claffey's Grove, Crinken, as the site for an ambush. Following nightly vigils for over a week, a military lorry passed and the Volunteers opened fire and lobbed bombs. Three soldiers were wounded in the attack and immediately following it the Volunteers crossed the fields to the moat in Lord Plunket's demesne where they concealed their arms. Subsequently the military rounded up thirty men in Shankill and marched them, carrying shovels and picks, to Alley's River Road and Ballymahon where they dug trenches across the road. Other operations by the Volunteers around this period included the destruction of two British military ambulances in the goods yard; and in a raid on the telephone man's hut, telephone apparatus, tools and a bicycle were stolen.

During the years of the First World War there was a dramatic decline in the Gaelic League's activities as its members were otherwise engaged, but from January 1920 there was a notable upsurge of interest under the chairmanship of Father John Murnane, and the League in Bray was well supported. In 1920 the *Coisde Ceanntar Brí Chualann* was organised and nine classes were held weekly for adults and children and frequent lectures were given on historical, cultural and archaeological matters. Interest in the language was so extensive that concerts and Irish dramas played to capacity audiences.

Curfew was in operation throughout the winter of 1920 and anyone found outdoors after 10 p.m. without a pass was liable to be shot or arrested. One man standing by his door near the Town Hall was shot dead by the Back and Tans. During the activities of 1920–21 there was a series of raids by police and soldiers on the homes of IRA suspects and sympathisers. From 1 April 1921 there was an extension of the curfew from 8 p.m. to 5 a.m. Many locals were agitated by this curtailment of their freedom and there was mounting tension in the town.

In 1921 there were twenty RIC and twenty Black and Tans stationed between the barracks and the courthouse. With their strategic position these buildings were a virtual fortress, commanding a panoramic view of the river and Little Bray. The local IRA joined with other companies to stage a major assault on the stronghold. Heretofore, the only attacks had been by an occasional sniper who would keep the occupants in a state of nervousness and have them waste ammunition in returning fire. Following the initial sniper shots, Verey lights went up from the barracks and reinforcements came from Enniskerry and Kilpedder to support the RIC. Most newspaper reports of the period exaggerated the skirmishes. One account of an operation in which the IRA fired only twenty rounds stated that the barracks and courthouse had been surrounded by a large number of attackers and a determined effort had been made to capture them. Most of the IRA men, it stated, were concealed behind tombstones in the graveyard of Saint Paul's church where they maintained a heavy machine-gun attack. Members of the local company categorically denied that they ever fired from that position.

On the night of 18 April 1921 two bombs were thrown through the door of the courthouse. This was the signal to the IRA, armed with service rifles, to open fire on the two buildings from the cover of the golf links. The garrison returned fire with rifles and machine guns. Heavy fire was maintained in the direction of the attackers and also up the Main Street, where many shop windows were shattered. Very lights went up but it was almost two hours before the garrison ceased fire. Following the attack, the IRA commanding officer, Lieutenant Pat Brien, handed over the rifles to Tom Sutton and 'Lukey' Leggett who lived on the Dargle Road, for safe keeping. Later that night there were widespread arrests by the RIC. Many of the IRA men convicted during this period were imprisoned in Arbour Hill or the Curragh. Following this attack the army commandeered the Royal Hotel and established a military post with up to a hundred troops. With the internment of a large number of local IRA officers, Rory McDermott from Blackrock was appointed new commanding officer of the Bray Company. His instruction on arrival was to kill the head of the RIC, District Inspector Lowndes. Volunteers took up positions in doorways near the barracks for several nights but they never had the opportunity to carry out the order.

A later sniper incident on the garrison had unfortunate consequences for two Shankill men. Having fired several rounds from the golf links one morning, Josie Faulkner and Jack Sheehan retreated across the fields to Shankill. They were spotted by an ex-member of the RIC. Later that day while standing at Shankill Bridge with other men, a lorry load of RIC and Black and Tans from Bray surrounded and searched the group. Faulkner and Sheehan were taken to the barracks in Bray. Later, Faulkner's mother visited him and on leaving was asked if she would take her son's overcoat. The coat had been found on the route taken by the two men and Faulkner had denied that it was his. The recognition by his mother proved their link and the two men received a savage beating and a ten-year prison sentence.

During the greater part of the Troubles, a small group of active IRA men were on the run in the town, which was generally unsympathetic to their cause. One of the normal resting places for members on active service on the north side of the town was the first-class carriages at the railway siding near the Martello Tower. Others sought refuge in woods on the outskirts of the town. The O/C and other officers stayed at 31 Duncairn Avenue, the home of William Redmond, a journalist, who was not suspected by the authorities of being a supporter of the movement.

Controversy surrounded the Gaelic League *Feis* in 1921 in Bray and the homes of the two secretaries were searched. The British authorities stated that if a permit were sought permission to hold the *Feis* would be granted, but if not it would be prohibited. Gaelic League headquarters instructed that no permit should be sought for any of its functions. On the eve of the *Feis* it was announced that the truce was to begin officially on Monday 11 July, the day after the *Feis*. But in Bray the truce began with the *Feis*, the greatest gathering of Gaels in the town for years. Sinéad de Valera formally opened it under the guns of a lorry-load of British troops, but there were no incidents. The standard of the competitions was high and there was more Irish spoken amongst the huge attendance than at any other gathering on the esplanade.

In December 1921 the Treaty was signed and the internees were released from the Curragh. Local men were met at the bridge by a torch-lit procession and St Kevin's Brass and Reed Band played as bonfires illuminated the night sky. The following January the military vacated the Royal Hotel and soon afterwards the RIC left the courthouse and barracks. A meeting was called in the Town Hall by interested parties for the forming of a civic guard.

11

THE FREE STATE AND THE SECOND WORLD WAR

By the beginning of the twentieth century, the population of Bray had risen to 7,500 and the area was developed on several levels. It was undoubtedly the leading upmarket resort in the country and one of the best in these islands, as it abounded with natural amenities along with man-made improvements. The railway company ran a half-hourly train service until midnight every day.

The amusement committee was engaged in the organisation of top-class entertainment, with guests including the likes of Percy French. Some of the most popular shows were Will C. Pepper's White Coons and George Rapley's Troup who performed on the esplanade bandstand. Firework displays took place on the esplanade also. The town offered facilities for boating, yachting, bathing, fishing, tennis and a splendid golf club. Change began to gradually manifest itself and there was not the same drive for greater improvement or further exploitation of the resort's natural potential.

In 1898 under legislation the Local Government (Ireland) Act was introduced, under which the township area acquired an urban district status. At the first (statutory) meeting of the council in the Town Hall on 23 January 1899, Councillor James E. McCormick was elected the first chairman. The meeting also elected members for the harbour committee, general purposes committee and electric light committee. A report was read to the meeting from the superintendent medical officer of health stating that 'for the four weeks ending 31 December 1898 the total birth-rate in Bray Urban Sanitary District was 12.7 per 1,000 living. The death rate from all causes was 7.9 per 1,000 living.' The chairman of the council was authorised to see the bank manager about the necessary overdraft for carrying on business of the council.

The new council placed more emphasis on basic essentials and abandoned many progressive schemes already in hand, which had been designed to preserve and extend the fashionable tourism dimension of the town. The councillors were more pre-occupied with improving drainage and sanitary arrangements and with building schemes such as the construction of artisans' dwellings, which accounted for the bulk of the town's expenditure between 1900 and 1914. One overdue improvement was the demolition of a number of poor artisans' cabins in Little Bray and the introduction to the town in 1900 of the provisions of the Housing of the Working Class Act (1895), whereby new streets containing about a hundred artisans' dwellings were erected on the Commons. They were Dargan Street, Maitland Street and Ardee Street. A new street was also constructed to the west of the Town Hall, adjacent to the Main Street. Connolly and Saint Kevin's Square were built in Purcell's Fields. In 1909 the principal alterations were the extension of Galtrim Road to join Adelaide Road and the opening of Kingsmill Road into the extension. Additional housing was urgently needed, as by 1911 the population had risen to 8,142.

Bray was linked to electric light in 1904 when a generator was erected, powered by a head of water from the River Dargle. Nearby Kingstown was slow to realise the advantages of electricity and many houses there were not wired until the late 1920s. The Bray Electric Company, which proved a dependable source of income, lit the seafront from its own works that supplied current to the entire town. In July 1912 an explosion at the works killed one man, Christopher Coates, and a second man, J. Souter, was seriously injured, losing both legs.

In 1899, with the establishment of the Urban District Council with new powers for improvement, taxation rates rose to 6s. By 1914 the valuation of the town had increased to £30,000 and taxation was bringing in considerable revenue. That year a rate of 7s in the pound was struck. The harbour showed poor returns for the initial investment and in later years was to become a burden on the taxpayers. By 1943 the harbour had ceased to operate for commercial purposes.

Living conditions amongst the poor of Little Bray in the early part of the century were described as primitive and cholera was widespread. In one year Bray Penny Dinners served almost 6,000 dinners in their depot in the forge in Castle Street. Class distinction and appalling snobbery existed on a wide scale, based on position and address.

In 1900 skilled workers could earn wages averaging 35s per week, while unskilled workers were expected to feed and house their families on an income averaging 20s per week. They also experienced greater insecurity and longer periods of unemployment. Working-class spending on drink only served to deepen their level of misery. By 1904 one in eight suffered from tuberculosis, a disease which thrived on inadequate food, overcrowded accommodation and damp conditions. Women were forced to take in washing for the gentry. Others got seasonal work binding oats on farms on the perimeter of the town. There was little else in the way of employment.

Conditions frequently deteriorated as a result of serious flooding in the Little Bray area. In one particularly disastrous flood on 26 August 1905 the river burst its banks and water rose between 6 and 11ft higher than normal. The 400 families (about 2,000 people) rendered homeless were given refuge in the Town Hall, the courthouse, the Royal Hotel and Sunnybank Inn. One man, James Plunkett, was drowned and many homes and properties were damaged. Lord Meath appealed for subscriptions with great success through the press. Amongst the contributors was the Royal Family, who sent a generous donation. By an ironic coincidence on 26 August 1986 the Dargle River burst its banks causing major flooding in the Little Bray area, eighty-one years to the day since the other devastating flood.

Soon trade unions were formed to better conditions for skilled workers, the Amalgamated Society of Carpenters and Joiners in 1890 being the earliest on record. A branch of the Irish Transport and General Workers' Union was established in Bray in 1911, four years after its foundation. The same year 'Big Jim' Larkin addressed a meeting of local members in the People's Park. The Irish Transport and General Workers' Union became involved in strikes at St Paul's Church and the Church of the Most Holy Redeemer, where construction was in progress. Other groups saw the benefits to be derived from organised action, and soon trade unions were formed amongst dockers, carters, cranesmen and coalmen. During the 1913 strike a relief centre was set up in the Old Castle in Castle Street to distribute food and clothes to the needy. Pressure on workers in all trades increased with the great strike and depression and the resulting shortages and soaring prices. On a proposal from the railwaymen's union, meetings were organised to co-ordinate activity among the various unions for their mutual protection.

A conference held in Bray Town Hall in April 1917, attended by delegates from all the unions from Greystones to Blackrock, decided to set up the Bray and Kingstown Trades and Labour Council. That council continues to operate to the present day under the title Bray and District Trades Union Council. During that era workers' trade union membership and political allegiance were the same.

While one section of the town was experiencing great deprivation a remarkable sporting personality named Sir Stanley Cochrane was adding an extra dimension to his large estate at Woodbrook. The flourishing mineral water company of Cantrell and Cochrane founded by his father had made him a wealthy man. He was a cricket enthusiast with the finance to indulge in patronage of the most lavish kind. In 1907 he established a first-class ground, complete with an elegant pavilion overlooking it, known as Woodbrook Club and Ground. He brought over world-class teams including the South Africans, Australians, Indians and a Yorkshire team captained by the great C.B. Fry. In addition he maintained a team at Woodbrook which included some eminent professionals. Cochrane was one of the first men in Ireland to take an interest in motoring and owned a fleet of expensive cars including two Rolls-Royces.

During his cricketing years, he was also deeply involved in music. Behind Woodbrook House he built what he originally intended as an indoor cricket pitch but later transformed it into an opera house. He was responsible for bringing over the famous Nellie Melba and the Quinlan Opera Company. The cricket weeks at Woodbrook were famous throughout Britain as well as Ireland, but such vast expenditure could not be maintained indefinitely and the cricket ended in 1912. Next Sir Stanley turned his attention to golf and had a course made on land on the far side of the railway line. So eager was the response that he decided to extend the scope by forming a club which he registered under the Clubs Act and for which there was a membership fee of 4 guineas per annum. Soon it became prestigious to be a member of the Woodbrook Club and when the nine-hole course opened seventy-one people joined.

In the 1918 general election Bray was part of the Wicklow/Kildare constituency and the five members returned were Robert Barton, the O'Mahony, J.R. Etchingham (who was in jail), H. Parker Keene and D.C. Cogan. Following their victory in the election Sinn Féin decided to establish their own parliament, the Dáil Éireann. Other non-Sinn Féin Irish MPs were invited to join them and abstain from Westminster. Only twenty-seven Sinn Féiners were available to attend the first session on the Mansion House on 21 January 1919. By the second session of the Dáil on 1 April 1919 Lloyd George had ordered the release of the Sinn Féin internees. At this meeting Éamon de Valera was elected President and Robert Barton Minister for Agriculture. In the next general election on 19 May 1920 Barton was returned for Wicklow and was joined by Art O'Connor, Domhnall Ó Buchalla, Erskine Childers and Christopher M. Byrne. Barton was one of the Irish delegation along with Michael Collins and Arthur Griffith at the Anglo-Irish Treaty negotiations in London on 11 October 1921. For the third Dáil election on 16 June 1922 De Valera and Michael Collins made a pact in which all candidates would stand as Sinn Féin and would form a power-sharing government. The five candidates elected for Wicklow were Barton, Byrne, James Everett, Richard Wilson and Hugh Colohan.

Following the Civil War that ended in May 1923, Bray was not to escape the subsequent high rate of unemployment and depression and also experienced an ingrained bitterness and division which was widespread between friends and families. In the first general election under the new constitution in August 1923, three members were returned for County

Wicklow: James Everett, Christopher M. Byrne and Richard Wilson. The first Wicklow TD actually living in Bray was James O'Toole of the Harbour Bar, elected as a Fianna Fáil deputy in the general election of March 1957.

For a town of its size and importance, Bray was unusual in never having a predominance of trade and industry. The principal industries were Smithson's Flour Mills and the Maltings in Mill Lane occupied by Watkins, Jameson and Pim & Co. For a period in the early part of the twentieth century trout fishing in the Dargle and its marketing in Dublin and London was a flourishing business. Several businessmen supplied the growing transport needs including Thompson's Carriage Works and Sawmills, Frank Dennehy's Carriage Works and Colliers which later expanded into the undertaking business. In the 1930s some larger factories opened in the town, including W. & E. W. Haughton, manufacturers of ink, gum and Felix polish in Little Bray and Solus Teo, the manufacturers of electric light bulbs at Corke Abbey. Some months after Sophie St John Whitty was appointed teacher of wood-carving at the newly opened Bray Technical School, she converted her carving class into the Bray Art Furniture Industry. The body subsequently developed into 'The Guild of Bray Woodworkers' and a special feature of their work was the artistic designs used in carving church furniture. Christ Church, Bray, displays some of the best examples of the Guild's work. The outbreak of war and the cancellation of orders led to the closure of the industry.

The Dublin and South Eastern Railway Company donated a site opposite the International Hotel for a war memorial for those who had lost their lives in the First World War. The memorial, in the form of a Celtic Cross, 22ft 6in high, cost £650 and had a plaque with the names of 150 soldiers who had lost their lives inscribed on it. A subscription list was opened for the monument, which was erected by Harrison & Sons.

A succession of wars at home and abroad between 1914 and 1923, followed by the setting up of the new state, greatly curtailed construction work and the previous progressive trend. There was no further major house-building by the local authority until the early 1930s when O'Byrne Road, Saint Bridget's Terrace, Saint Patrick's Square, Saint Cronan's Road, Saint Lawrence's Terrace, Kilmantain Park and Saint Columcille Terrace were erected. This period also saw the building of numerous orange-tiled bungalows that appear to have been peculiar to east coast resorts. In the mid-1930s private building began on the northern slopes of Bray Head. One of the only concessions the Urban District Council made to the seafront during this period was the erection in 1935 of six attractive kiosks along the esplanade.

Despite the lack of finance and facilities, a major transformation was to occur in an entire community in 1935. The Urban District Council declared many houses in Little Bray unfit for human habitation owing to bad drainage and a lack of proper sanitary arrangements. The houses were to be demolished and the inhabitants were given three weeks to vacate the properties and transfer to a new council housing scheme in the Vevay, where 268 houses had been constructed. Naturally there were mixed reactions from the residents, with much bitterness and resentment as many people were reluctant to leave their homes and refused to move. Eventually the enormous operation was completed and an entire community from beside the Dargle was rehoused in Wolfe Tone Square.

Bray, like the remainder of the country, did not escape the hardship and deprivation of the war years. The Emergency brought rationing, with restrictions becoming more stringent with the passage of time.

During the war years Bray was a garrison town with the Fifth Battalion of the regular army based in the International Hotel. They had outposts at Killarney Wood and Woodlands Hotel, Greystones. The area covered by the battalion extended to Shankill, Enniskerry, Kippure, Roundwood and Newcastle, and had to be serviced by 2,000 men. Many local men joined the British Army, the Royal Navy and the Royal Air Force while at home an army recruitment drive was launched for volunteers to join the auxiliary services. 4,000 men and women in the district were eligible to serve in the voluntary services but only 800 volunteered. The groups were the Local Defence Force (LDF) which was based in Rockbrae and had a maximum strength of 400, and the Air Raid Precautions (ARP), which was based in the sand-bagged fortified library which also housed communications and was the control centre. The warden service, with numbers varying from 150 to 200, also operated from the library. Their role was to enforce the blackout and in the event of an air raid direct people to cover. The Maritime Inscription Corps, consisting of about fifty men, were based at the harbour under military law and had the power to search boats. Other voluntary groups active during the Emergency were the Local Security Forces (LSF) stationed at the barracks, the Red Cross, the Order of Malta and Auxiliary Fire Service. A coast-watching service was established at Cable Rock along the Cliff Walk. The town was divided into five areas and twenty sections.

German bombers occasionally flew over the town. In February 1940 a bomb was dropped in Kilmacanogue but was defused. A mine washed up in Naylor's Cove in 1942 was blown up by the army.

One of the escape routes planned for the best known German spy, Günther Schütz, was through Bray. In 1942 while in Arbour Hill Military Prison, Schütz found a letter addressed to him under the toilet seat. In the letter a Charles McGuinness informed him that he had been detached to take him to France. The German Embassy had provided £3,000 for the purchase of a boat to make good his escape. The boat with a powerful Ford diesel engine was waiting in Bray Harbour but the operation was betrayed and was abandoned.

In the main there was little activity during the emergency and people grew bored and left the respective organisations. One beneficial effect of this period was that a sense of comradeship developed between all communities in the town. Many joint social events were organised between the voluntary bodies and many lasting friendships were formed.

During the war an interesting emergency civil engineering project was carried out by the Office of Public Works following the collapse of the sea wall during a severe storm on 16 November 1941. The break in the sea wall was followed rapidly by erosion of the land in front of the then CIE buffet and threatened a terrace of houses which then stood in the middle of the road. Another emergency scheme was devised and a hundred unemployed men were despatched to cut turf in Glencree bog to off-set the fuel shortage in Bray. At the end of the war a further plaque was added to the War Memorial, listing the names of those killed in action.

12

DEMISE OF THE
IRISH BRIGHTON

A steady transformation was to occur in Bray in the post-war period. In those changed social conditions the 'Brighton of Ireland' tag was to diminish, with a new expanding town emerging which was no longer upper-class and expensive. With large council housing schemes emerging, Bray was to become predominantly lower-middle and working-class in composition and as a tourist centre became a brash, gaudy resort. There was a tendency for almost two decades following the Second World War for a huge influx of visitors from England, Scotland, Wales and Northern Ireland to spend their annual holidays in Bray. Hotels and guesthouses were filled to capacity for three months each year and many private householders across a broad spectrum of society opened their homes for the lucrative bed and breakfast trade that helped offset their rates. Householders from the Meath Road to Little Bray to Wolfe Tone Square re-organised their lifestyles for the summer months to accommodate as many holidaymakers as possible. The small family run guest-houses were advertised as being easy on the pocket and accessible to the beach.

Bray was affected by a shift in summer holiday patterns moving from a fashionable resort to a miniature Blackpool with boarding houses, ice cream parlours, amusement arcades, one-armed bandits, paddle boats, sticks of rock and singing pubs. Bray Amusement Committee was re-formed to plan a series of entertainments for visitors. Amongst the wide range of activities they organised were band performances, dog shows, sandcastle competitions and open-air film shows and ceilis. The town had a variety of amenities to attract tourists: Williams Amusements on Bray Head, George Daniels' roadshow featuring drama and variety in Barry's Field, the aerial railway, the Fun Palace and Dawson's Amusement Arcades. Jack McDermott who had been the proprietor of a picture house in the Assembly Rooms opened the Arcadia Ballroom and turned it into one of the most successful dancing venues in the country. Music was provided by the popular Billy Carter and other artists who appeared there included Roy Orbison, Acker Bilk, Kenny Ball, the Royal and Miami Showbands and all the other leading showbands. Dancers were also catered for at the Eagle's Nest on Bray Head and to the music of Johnny Butler at Bar B in Woodbrook and cabaret in the International Hotel. Top performers of the calibre of Joe Loss, Victor Sylvester and Jack Doyle, 'The Gorgeous Gael', were featured in these venues. Val Doonican, Hal Roach and Harry Bailey all played the boards in Bray during their early careers. The emphasis was on popular entertainment and the air of sophistication nurtured by Dargan and his contemporaries rapidly disappeared.

This position was only temporary and from the mid-1960s a number of factors contributed to Bray's further deterioration as a premier holiday resort — cheap air travel, package holidays to the sun, increasing car ownership, a car ferry at Dun Laoghaire and escalating prices. The murder of a local youth in the mid-1960s and the subsequent unfavourable media publicity also had a detrimental effect. They all combined to entice the holidaymakers elsewhere and the tendency was to use Bray just for a brief stop-over or a day trip.

While the tourist dimension of the town was on the wane, building workers were kept in constant employment with an amalgam of new private and local authority housing estates. The construction of private housing estates throughout the town and on its perimeter was a noticeable feature of Bray from 1950. There was also an upsurge in council housing in the same period, most notably Saint Peter's Road, Palermo, Old Court, Ballywaltrim Heights and Fassaroe.

A number of new factories were built during the 1940s and 1950s the most significant being Industrial Yarns, housing an important textile industry. The factory was constructed on the site of the former Thompson's sandpit on the Dublin Road and a considerable amount of land reclamation was necessary before the building could proceed. Operating at maximum capacity the factory employed over one hundred people. Unfortunately, with a world-wide slump in nylon products, the factory experienced serious trading difficulties from the mid-1970s and the workforce was drastically reduced. Other small industries operating in Bray around this period included Kennymores, the sweet manufacturers in Back Street, Coughlan's toothpaste factory at the harbour and Coxon's wallpaper factory in the Old Mill. A local branch of the Chamber of Commerce was established in 1956.

The opening of Ardmore Studios in 1958 initially brought confidence and prestige, with stars of the calibre of James Cagney and Robert Mitchum filming at the studio. There were also spin-off benefits to hotels, restaurants, shops, coach hire and employment for tradesmen and extras.

The problems for Ardmore began in 1962 with a series of trade disputes and financial difficulties. Over the intervening years there were a number of owners and receivers appointed. In 1974 the government purchased the studio and the film director John Boorman was appointed chairman. Even this constructive move did not prevent further problems and in 1982 the Minister for Industry and Commerce, Albert Reynolds, closed the studio.

In the Boghall area several industrial estates were established, attracting a number of diverse industries to the town. The most successful of these were A.O. Smith, the electric motor manufacturers and the German-based computer firm of Nixdorf. The Arcadia Ballroom was bought by Amalgamated Wholesalers Limited as a warehouse. In 1974 unemployment in the town stood at 800.

The once lively Albert Walk has deteriorated in recent years with some premises lying idle. Coastal erosion has been responsible for the destruction of many amenities including Naylor's Cove, sections of the Cliff Walk, the Back Strand, the old harbour bridge, the collapse of the lighthouse and continual undermining of the harbour walls and promenade. The lead mines, brick works on Killarney Road and sandpits within the town have been long worked out. Fires destroyed the International Hotel, Arcadia, Royal Marine Hotel, the Old English-style park lodge and Coxon's wallpaper factory, while the castle in Castle Street was demolished and the Turkish Baths made way for a shopping centre. Despite massive urban development, the town, and the seafront to a greater degree, have staunchly managed to retain their distinctive character with most of their Victorian architectural heritage still in a healthy state of preservation.

After a serious flood in November 1965 in which the weir was broken and a portion of the river wall collapsed, a flood prevention scheme was implemented at a cost of £120,000. It involved lowering the river-bed and rebuilding walls. In December 1969 the UDC drew up a formal town plan setting out its development policy for the preservation and improvement of Bray as a tourist centre, a dormitory town, and a centre for light industry, in that order. Also in the late 1960s the first stage of a major sewerage scheme for the town was commenced.

13

BRAY CHURCHES

When Strongbow granted Sir Walter de Ridelisford the barony of Bray, de Ridelisford felt obliged to share his lands with the Church. He founded a convent for nuns canonesses of Saint Augustine in Grange, County Kildare, and gave them benefices of churches and chapels in Bray. This convent was entitled to receive rectorial tithes. As their part of the agreement the nuns had to present a clergyman to administer the parish with the title of vicar. This became a permanent vicarage and the incumbent could only be removed for an indiscretion. From 1200 Bray had a succession of vicars presented by the nuns of Grange.

During de Ridelisford's reign there were several other religious houses on the southern side of Bray river, including the abbeys of St Thomas, St Mary the Virgin and St John of Tristledermot, with tenements which had been granted to them by de Ridelisford. These tenements were used by the monks to carry on trade with the Irish inhabitants in the mountains. To finance this trade a weekly market was held each Thursday. In the Abbeys of St Thomas and St Mary one of the chief commodities produced was firewood which was conveyed to Dublin by sea in small boats, which could navigate the shallow waters of the River Liffey and land their cargoes close to the monasteries. Even prior to this, tradition has it that Corke Abbey, the seat of Sir Edward Wingfield Verner, occupied the site of a Celtic monastic settlement founded by Saint Curcagh of Cill Curcaighe.

In 1535 Henry VIII sent a commissioner to the bishops of Meath and Kildare and the Master of the Rolls to suppress the Nunnery of Grange, evict the nuns and confiscate their property. By this despotic act, Henry became the Rector of Bray and until the disestablishment of the patronage the rectory was vested in the crown. Henry's action may have disrupted the administration of the church but not the worship of the people, which continued at a consistently high level. Under the reign of Elizabeth I, from

1559, there was an even greater effort to destroy Catholicism with the seizure of churches, mass being proscribed, priests being hounded and the organisation of the church disintegrating.

In 1615 Archbishop Matthews assembled a secret Synod in Kilkenny in the hope of stemming this tide. One of the objectives of the synod was to re-organise parishes. Amongst these was the small parish of Bray, which was merged with the larger parish of Stagonil, Kilcroney, Templecarrig, Killruddery and Kilmacanogue into one single parish under one priest. The parish became known as the parish of Kilmacanogue and Bray with Father Dermot Byrne as its first parish priest.

During the seventeenth century in Bray there was a large attendance of military families at Church of Ireland services; there is also a conspicuous military presence in the records of births, marriages and deaths. In 1615, when Maurice Byrne was Vicar of Bray, he preached his sermons in Irish, and had the Book of Common Prayer translated into Irish – this suggests a native Irish element in the congregation. In its religious composition Bray had a preponderance of Catholics – a ratio of three Catholics to one Protestant – but the Protestants tended in the main to be of a higher social status than Catholics who were mainly of the poorer labouring class. Parish registers for the Church of Ireland indicated that the Protestant religion was not confined to any one class – gentry, farmers, nobility, militia, traders, craftsmen, fishermen and labourers were all represented. However, names tended to be predominantly English, which would suggest a colonist rather than a native Irish origin. 'Protestant' names featured almost exclusively in property transactions. This is easily explained: firstly, penal legislation against Catholic land ownership dated from exactly this period, when property deeds began to appear in significant numbers. Secondly, with a few exceptions (e.g. the Walshes of Old Connaught, the Ledwidges of Killarney and the Eustaces of Old Court), the Catholic population was of low social status and unable to afford a church for the area. Later when the church was built they were unable to pay the 40s per annum rent or to support a curate in addition to the parish priest.

Prior to the opening of a Catholic chapel in Bray, priests had nowhere to celebrate Mass and were supported by catholic gentry who provided facilities for them to administer the Sacraments. In 1630, when Archbishop Buckley made his report on the Dublin Diocese, he stated that several priests and friars lived in Old Connaught as guests of James Walshe. The record states: 'Bray – Dermot Byrne, a mass priest, celebrates mass sheltered by Mrs Joan Eustace, a widow, in her mansion at Old Connaught, Bray.' The Walshe family also supported a teacher, Garret Warren, to educate their children. Although the Walshes maintained a priest until they disappeared from the area around 1760, priests supported by the gentry did not continue in Great Bray.

A decree issued in 1704 stated that, while no bishop, vicar general or regular was allowed in the kingdom under penalty of high treason, one priest was allowed to each parish, provided he was registered, but was to have no successor. This meant on his death there would be no Catholic representative in the parish. The first priest registered was Father Fitzsimons. The register read 'Richard Fitzsimons living at Kilmillen, aged 45, parish priest of Delgany, Powerscourt, Kilmacangoue and Bray. Ordained in 1682 in Flanders by Archbishop of Cambray. Sureties Peter White, Matthew Robinet, £50 each.'

Records are sketchy for this period but it can be assumed that he remained as parish priest until he was succeeded by Father Stephen Cavannagh in 1735. Father Arthur O'Neill was appointed parish priest in 1760 and died on 22 May 1794. Canon Christopher Callaghan was appointed parish priest of Kilmacanogue and Bray in 1795. One of his successors was the Very Reverend Canon John Miley, in whose arms Daniel O'Connell died. The records only contain five names and also state for a long period there 'was no priest in Bray'. From the end of the eighteenth century Bray was divided between two parishes, one being in Loughlinstown, extending from Blackrock to Bray River and from the sea to the mountains of Glencullen; the other being Kilmacanogue, extending from Bray River to Greystones and from the sea to Glencree. The parish church for Bray was in Kilmacanogue where the parish priest resided, services were held there and parishioners had to travel on foot or horseback. Kilmacanogue was then a more populated area than it is today.

In 1760 a small chapel was constructed to the west of Old Connaught village at Jubilee but collapsed in 1780. The next chapel to be built was at Crinken, 2 miles from the town; this was used by the Catholics of Little Bray until the chapel was built in Great Bray. The chapel in Main Street, built as a chapel of ease for Kilmacanogue, for which records first appear in 1792, was apparently never completed. By 1800, with a rent of £2 annually, it had run into arrears because of the poverty of the parishioners, and they were evicted by the landlord John Donnelan, who removed the roof of the church and built a house in front of it. Father Christopher Callaghan from Finglas came to Bray as a curate in 1792 and was promoted to parish priest three years later. On 7 April 1801 he made an entry in the parochial register: 'Rev Peter Synott left me this year, the scarcity of the times being great. The area suffered from husbandry neglect and the resulting depopulation.'

In 1809, aided by subscriptions from leading Protestants in the area, the chapel was completed and mass celebrated there every Sunday. This was a small chapel built behind the houses in the Main Street. By 1823 the town's Catholic population had increased to such a degree that the existing church was considered too small to accommodate the congregation. On 17 November that year Father Callaghan died and was buried in

Kilmacanogue. His successor Father James Doyle insisted that a larger church must be built. The old church was demolished and Father Doyle laid the foundation stone for the 'Great New Chapel of Bray' in 1824 on the same site.

Church of the Most Holy Redeemer

The new building cost £1,600. A great deal of this cost was born once again by local Protestants. It was an ambitious enterprise at that time. Father Doyle moved his residence and the headquarters of the parish to Bray. General Sir George Cockburn of Shanganagh presented an altar-piece to the new church. Father Doyle, who died aged forty-seven before its completion in June 1826, achieved much in his short period as parish priest, including a parochial residence and schools at Curtlestown and Enniskerry. The church was a plain oblong building 95ft long by 30ft high. It was weather-boarded on the south side and roughcast all the way round. Some houses blocked its façade from the road but these were later purchased and demolished.

The church in Enniskerry was built in 1860 replacing what was described as a barn at the rear of a public house. Father Thomas O'Dwyer was its first parish priest. The church at Blacklion was erect in 1867 and a temporary church known as the 'Iron Church' was erected in Greystones at a cost of £400. Prior to this, the priest had to travel from Bray on horseback over the Gap of Windgates to say mass every Sunday. Around 1860 Enniskerry and Kilmacanogue were separated from Bray. Greystones split off from Bray in 1908 when the new church was constructed there.

In 1850 the church in Main Street was extended in granite with 33ft added to the nave's length and a tower erected. This project was completed four years later at a cost of £2,000. Catholic records show a steady increase in congregations from 2,745 in 1834 to 3,395 in 1891. In 1896 it was agreed to further enlarge the church to cope with the growing numbers. The architect W.H. Byrne drew up plans for the chancel, apse, transepts, one bay, the nave and sacristy. The estimate of £12,000 by contractor Michael Meade and Son was first thought to be too expensive but work went ahead. Between 1896 and 1902 a parish magazine entitled *The Bray Catholic Monitor* was published. In 1898 the chancels and side altars were decorated by Signor Edward Buccini, a Neapolitan artist living in Bray. In May 1898 the altars were consecrated and in July of that year the new church was opened. The Archbishop presided at the opening ceremony, the Bishop of Limerick preached and the Bishop of Canea pontificated. The occasion was recorded on a marble slab in the apse.

A free grant of land for a presbytery was given by the Earl of Pembroke round this time, with one condition: that the house had to be begun within six months. The original estimate was £2,000 but this was decreased by

£200 with the supervision of a member of the building committee. During the course of the work, it was discovered that the foundations of the south wall of the transept would interfere with the existing stable of Mr Merrigan. He assigned his lease in return for a new stable built for £374. Six stained-glass windows, the gift of Mrs R. O'Byrne, were fitted in the apse in 1897. In March 1900 there was an addition to the church when 100ft of frontage was secured from the Earl of Pembroke at a rent of £5 per annum. The grounds were excavated, laid out and enclosed by a wall and iron railings. By 1914 the organ gallery was erected and the organ installed but further plans contemplated for church improvements were dropped due to the outbreak of war.

Relations between the religious denominations were exemplary, with local Protestants contributing to the new Catholic church and also the bulk of the annual collection for the maintenance of Catholic parochial schools, founded in 1820. There is even a reference to the Rector of Bray acting as collector in the Catholic church at Sunday mass. Both denominations threw themselves wholeheartedly behind the O'Connell campaign for Catholic emancipation. One proselytiser, the Revd Robert Daly of Powerscourt parish (later to become Bishop of Cathel and Water), for a time in the 1820s did his utmost to break up the spirit of co-operation between the two faiths by stirring up anti-Catholic feeling. He attempted to hinder Catholic masters on their way to school, evicted tenants of Lord Powerscourt without his knowledge and did his utmost to exert his influence on the parish of Bray. This prompted a letter from the parish priest to Daniel O'Connell in July 1829, denouncing Revd Daly and referring to the 'utmost unanimity' which had existed before Daly's arrival. Fortunately the Daly example was not followed.

St Paul's Church
Until the beginning of the nineteenth century the only Protestant church for miles around Bray was St Paul's, built in 1609. The Ecclesiastical Union of the Established Church included Old Connaught and Rathmichael in this parish. Since 1280 St Paul's had been the centre of the rural deanery, called the Deanery of Bre, which extended from Stillorgan and Kill-of-the-Grange in the north to Newcastle and Killadreenan in the south.

It is almost certain that there was a church on the same site before this date as Archbishop Alan, a pre-Reformation antiquarian, recalled in his *Repertorium Viride* written in 1530 that the Church of Bre was anciently called the Parochial Church of Derichat. Prior to that we find the de Ridelisford created the town of Bre in 1174 by building his feudal castle to the west of St Paul's churchyard. Samuel Lewis' *Topographical Dictionary* stated that the present church was built in 1609. It is apparent both from the testimony of Archbishop Jones and the royal commissioners who conducted the 'Royal Visitation' in 1615 that the church was then in good repair and that services were conducted in it. The tithes of the parish amounted to £230 and Bray, Old Connaught and Rathmichael to £340. Between 1765 and 1770 storm damage to the church was repaired at a cost of £200. At the same time new pews were installed by donations from various parishioners to whom use of them was allocated. In 1775 a small pointed spire was erected on the tower at a cost of £11 7s 6d. An old print, dating from the end of the eighteenth century, shows the church as consisting only of the present nave and tower, and with this spire upon the tower. In 1818 the church was enlarged with the addition of two transepts which formed the building into a 'T' shape. To undertake this work they received a loan of £1,020 from the late Board of the First Fruits. In 1824 Kilternan was detached from Bray and annexed to Kilgobbin. That same year William Conyngham Plunket, son of the first Lord Plunket, was appointed rector of St Paul's. Two years later Rathmichael was annexed to Bray. The spire lasted until 1833, when it was removed, and the battlements and pinnacles were substituted. In 1862 Reverend Canon George Digby Scott, the historian and author of the *Stones of Bray*, was appointed rector. In 1869 the long east wall was pierced by three arches and the church was completely refurbished for about £1,460. That year the church was dedicated on All Saint's Day and given the name St Paul's. By then it was no longer the parish church, having been reduced to the status of a chapel of ease when Christ Church was consecrated in 1863 and made the parish church of Bray. The most remarkable monument was a large Celtic cross, erected to the memory of William, eleventh Earl of Meath, in 1887.

Christ Church

The number of Catholics in Bray parish declined from 3,554 to 3,395 between 1861 and 1891, while in the same period the Church of Ireland population rose from 664 to 1,328. Catholic families in general were unable to afford the new houses being built at the time. In the years following 1850, in order to cope with the demand, the idea was mooted to build a new parish church for the Church of Ireland. When a site, on the rock of Bray, on the new Church Road, was offered by Lord Herbert of Lea, a committee was formed to raise funds and carry out the project. The rector of the parish, Archdeacon Whately, was supported in the promotion of the scheme especially by the Earl and Countess of Meath. Their efforts contributed to the raising of £4,000 which almost equalled the amount granted by the ecclesiastical commissioner, enabling the shell of the church and the base of the tower to be erected. The design was drawn up by the Victorian architects Messrs Carpenter and Slater of London. Progress was slow but finally, on St James's Day, 25 July 1863, Christ Church was consecrated by the Bishop of Killaloe, Dr FitzGerald. The building then consisted of a nave and chancel. In the original design the sanctuary was to be extended by another 30ft, but was reduced to save expense. The church was plain and unadorned when it was first consecrated but scarcely a year had passed before some gifts were added to it. Later the impressive tower and spire were added. A fine peal of bells were hung by Taylors of Loughborough in 1881. Nearly every year one of the stained-glass windows, which illustrate scenes of the life of Christ, beginning with the nativity, was given as a memorial. An ambitious number of schemes were undertaken during the 1870s and 1880s, including the building of a rectory on a site given by the Earl of Pembroke and the erection of a parochial hall on Novara Road.

The Methodist Church

The earliest premises used by the Methodists in Bray were a lecture hall and manse built by Reverend Adam Averell in 1795. From 1845, services were conducted in a room in Eglinton Road by Reverend Thomas C. Maguire, until the church was built in 1863 on Florence Road.

St Andrew's Presbyterian Church

The Irish Evangelical Church was founded in 1814 for the purpose of carrying out mission work in Ireland. Bray was one of the first areas of activity for the society and they held services in the home of a Mr Beggs in Little Bray on the corner of Old Connaught Road. The house later became Wilde's coach factory. Students for the ministry attended and conducted weekly services in the courthouse. The attendance at these services was so encouraging that in 1817 'a plain but neat place of worship was built' behind No.88 Main Street. In 1840 there was a sharp decline in attendance with about twenty persons at public worship, and the presbytery deemed it unwise to maintain the church for so small a number. Mr John Powell, the assistant minister, also taught school in what is Novara House. Following the appointment of Mr James Patterson to Bray in 1849, the congregation steadily grew and prospered. During the remainder of the century there was a small but steady influx of Scottish settlers into this part of the country. Some came to set up in business, others acted as land stewards in the surrounding estates. Bray had also become a popular seaside resort, not only for Dubliners but for people farther afield. These factors helped to bring about a steady increase in the size and importance of the congregation. The old church in the Main Street was deemed too small to accommodate the congregation, so in 1858, the present building on Quinsboro Road was erected; it opened for public worship on 12 September. The opening was conducted by the famous Dr Henry Cooke of Belfast.

In those days singing in Presbyterian churches was unaccompanied, as any form of musical instrument was prohibited by order of the General

Assembly. The choir was led by a precentor. In 1878, in spite of this law, the Bray congregation introduced a harmonium. The following is an extract from the *Report of Dublin Presbytery's Visitation to Bray Congregation* on 6 January 1878: 'Regretted that the minister and his people have introduced the harmonium into public worship – as they thought, for the good of the congregation – but would urge them to make another effort to comply with the instruction of the general assembly.' In compliance with the request, the use of the harmonium was abandoned. Revd Henry Patterson Glenn, who became rector in 1892, was a generous benefactor of the society. In 1940 the then minister was associated with the Catholic parish priest in the establishment of a turf scheme, the purpose of which was to give greater employment in the district.

Kilbride Church
The foundation stone for the small Church of Ireland church at Kilbride, near Kilcroney, was laid in 1858. The church was opened on 9 June 1859 with Revd L.H. Streane as its first rector.

The Quakers
The Society of Friends, better known as the Quakers, had no meeting place in Bray until the Turkish Baths were turned into the Assembly Rooms. Prior to that John Barrington of Fassaroe, who was a member of the Society, used to drive each Sunday in a covered car to a meeting in Monkstown.

St Fergal's Church
Around 1870 the Irish Franciscans discussed the possibility of acquiring a new site for their noviciate because their friary at Drogheda was deemed unsuitable. It was proposed to them that they should buy a site with a house at Ballywaltrim, outside Bray, for a noviciate and house of studies. A number of friars and the canonical visitor of the province were against it because of the expenses involved, the possibility of being refused a parish church and the untraditional suggestion of housing novices and students in the same friary. Eventually the plan was dropped when the Protestant owner of the site refused to sell it to a religious order. A century later, in 1974, history repeated itself when the Archbishop of Dublin, Dr Dermot Ryan, requested the Friars Minor to take pastoral responsibility for the Ballywaltrim area, which was growing rapidly as a new suburb of Bray. The invitation was accepted and in 1975 Father Roderic Ahearne OFM was appointed by the archbishop to the parish of Our Lady Queen of Peace as a curate with special responsibility for Ballywaltrim. In August 1975 the Provincial Chapter, Father John Bosco O'Byrne OFM arrived to assist him. The area assigned to them already had seven housing estates but no school,

no church and no presbytery. For some months mass was celebrated in a shed or in the open air before a large wooden structure was erected to serve as a temporary church. In May 1976 Ballywaltrim was canonically made into an independent parish, dedicated to Saint Fergal, the eighth-century Irish saint.

St Peter's Church

St Peter's Catholic Church, Little Bray, was built in 1837 as a replacement for the church at Crinken, which had fallen down. It is a small, unpretentious structure hidden from the public road and built to the design followed in penal days. The popular Father James Healy was transferred from Dublin to Bray, as a curate, by Archbishop Cullen and in 1867 he became administrator of Little Bray. The area was then in County Dublin and the remainder of Bray in County Wicklow. Previously Little Bray was part of Kingstown. There were 230 dwellings in the parish with 1,168 inhabitants. In 1886 Cabinteely was added to the parish of Little Bray. Eight years later Little Bray was reunited with 'Big' Bray and remained so until it was reconstituted as a parish again in 1975. The church was renowned for its classical reredos and high altar. The Stations of the Cross were painted by George Collie, RHA. Beside the church Saint Peter's Cemetery was blessed and opened in 1842 by the Most Reverend William Walsh, Bishop of Halifax, who had been until his consecration a few days previously, curate in the parish. In 1905 when all available space even most of the walks had been used for graves, adjoining land was purchased for a new cemetery. Forty years later a further extension had to be added.

Our Lady Queen of Peace

A public meeting was held on 5 January 1945 to open a fund for a new church in the Vevay. Canon Moriarty, parish priest of the Most Holy Redeemer, presided. A picturesque two-acre site was a gift of the Presentation Brothers to the parish. The church, dedicated to Our Lady Queen of Peace, was opened on 15 December 1946 by the Archbishop of Dublin, Most Reverend Dr McQuaid. It became a parish church in 1951.

14

EDUCATION AND SCHOOLS

The first recorded parochial school in Bray was on Seapoint Road and known officially as the 'Bray Roman Catholic Male and Female Parochial Schools'. The school, a single-storey building, was opened on 20 June 1820 and the parish priest, Father James Doyle, had it refurbished in 1824. In fact it was two schools, one for boys and another for girls. By 1834 there were nine Catholic schools in the parish including three 'pay' schools that were attended by fifty-seven boys and twenty-five girls. An infants' school was held in a spacious building erected by Viscount Powerscourt and supported by contributions. The Little Bray Male and Female Schools were erected in 1874 on the site of an older school which collapsed during renovation. It housed both boys and girls until Ravenswell Girls' School was opened in 1901. The girls section of the Seapoint School also closed that year.

The fact that over 30 per cent of the population was illiterate was one of the main reasons that prompted Father Christopher Callaghan to establish the Little Bray School. The only form of education for the poorer classes was the primitive Seapoint Road school or hedge schools. For the better off there were 'pay' catholic schools and schools of a non-denominational nature acceptable to Catholics. Father Callaghan formed a committee to set up this new school with himself as chairman and John Quin, proprietor of Quin's Hotel, as vice-president.

For the first fifteen years of their existence the Bray Poor Schools were not in the national educational system as it did not become operative until 1831. The schools were owned by the parish and their main source of income was a nineteenth century phenomenon known as the Charity Sermon – an annual social event. *The Freeman's Journal* carried this notice on 20 July 1820: 'A sermon to be preached in Bray Chapel by Revd C.V. Dowling OSD in aid of the extensive male and female schools of that town in which nearly 400 children receive the benefits of a literary and moral education, are trained up to habits of industry and virtue, and qualified to fill their humble spheres of life with prosperity and decorum'. For the first fifty years there was only one teacher, who had the help of an assistant. The average salary of teachers around this period was £16 13s 7d per annum. By 1866 their average salary had risen to £52 a year. The only adverse comments about the school in the mid-nineteenth century concerned the lack of discipline, cleanliness and neatness amongst the pupils.

In 1867 Bray was the country's most fashionable resort and the new parish priest, Dr Walter Lee, nephew of two archbishops of Dublin and former secretary of Maynooth college, felt that the schools were in deplorable state for such an important town. The great philanthropic 'inventor' of the headline copybook, Vere Foster, expressed similar sentiments in a comment in the visitor's book: '12 May 1866. Visited after school hours. Bray might afford a better school.'

Dr Lee set plans in motion for a new school. Various fund-raising events were organised and by early 1880 the school project was completed at a cost of £1,220 8s 1½d. It was known as Big Bray's National School and was situated on the Herbert Road (the present Little Flower Hall). Messrs Byrne and O'Neill were the architects and Stephen Breen the contractor. There is evidence of school fees in the register ranging from 4s to £2. The basis on which they were paid is not clear but fees were abolished under the Education Act of 1892. By the mid-1890s there were three teachers in the school, Dr Terence Clarke, principal and founder member of the Irish National Teacher Organisation, James Whiteside and George R. O'Connor. In 1906 a strike occurred amongst the boys.

Every day at midday two boys were sent to Ravenswell Convent with a brush handle and a large container to collect cocoa. They then had to transport the full hot container suspended on the brush handle back to the school. The cocoa was distributed to the boys with slices of bread.

The period 1914–23 was marked in various ways in the record of the school. A war bonus was paid to the teachers and many of the pupils' fathers were described as soldiers. A more effective compulsory school attendance law was introduced in 1926 with the onus of enforcement placed on the gardaí. This factor, together with the growth of the town, brought a rapid increase in numbers. By 1929 the school was badly overcrowded, and additional classes had to be accommodated in a house in Brighton Terrace. It became obvious that larger premises would be required.

St Cronan's National School

On 19 September 1932 Saint Cronan's National School was officially opened on Convent Hill. The new premises cost £10,000 and there was a debt of £3,863. A public meeting was held by Canon Bowden, parish priest, in the school on 13 October with Dr Wall, co-adjutor Bishop of Dublin, present. James McGarry, NT Principal of St Peter's, proposed that a list be opened. The clergy gave £500 and the other large contributions amounted to £900. Patrick McDonnell, affectionately known as 'Paddy Mac', was the first headmaster.

St Peter's National School

In 1874 St Peter's National School was constructed beside St Peter's Church and served as a junior boys' school for Little Bray district. In the original building the upper floor was assigned to girls and the lower floor to boys. The Sisters of Charity gave religious instruction in the school. A section of the building was used as a savings bank for the parish of Bray, Delgany and Powerscourt. The boys were drilled in the yard all year round by an ex-army officer, wielding a blackthorn stick. Later a new larger school was built in the Palermo housing estate.

St Laurence's High School

St Laurence's High Class Intermediate School was established as a boys' post-primary school, but it only functioned from September 1906 to January 1909. There followed a void in which no secondary facilities existed for boys in the district until the opening of Presentation College.

Presentation College

The Presentation Brothers acquired Charles Putland's residence at the north side of Bray Head and opened a boys' school there for primary and secondary education in 1920. The order was founded by Edmund Ignatius Rice (he also founded the Irish Christian Brothers). He had given up his personal property and eminent status in society to found religious communities of Brothers dedicated to the education of the young. At that time there were 150 boys on the school roll. In 1924 the old stables were reconstructed to provide additional classrooms. The second extension in 1956 consisted of an assembly hall and more classrooms. (The primary school has since closed.) The number of pupils on the roll was then 350. The third extension in 1970 provided the new college, the swimming pool and the new sports fields. The roll had by then risen to 700 boys.

St Brendan's College

St Brendan's College was opened on 5 September 1956 by the Irish Christian Brothers to provide secondary education for boys, with Brother Flynn as the first principal. The school was originally situated in Walcott House on Old Connaught Road, a former hotel purchased by the brothers as a temporary school. They subsequently moved to a new school built on Dublin Road, Woodbrook, with adjoining playing pitches.

Meath Industrial School

The Meath Industrial School for Girls was founded by William, Earl of Meath, in 1892 and was supported by a government grant of 5s per week for each child, supplemented by subscriptions and donations from the public. The Earl took a great deal of interest in the school, which was managed by a committee of ladies and gentlemen. It was licensed to accommodate a hundred girls, who left the school at the age of sixteen and were provided with 'situations' (employment), having been carefully trained in all branches of domestic science. This building was to have a chequered history, becoming the Duke of Connaught Hospital and then the Royal Drummond Institution for orphaned daughters of deceased soldiers. In 1944 it was taken over by the Loreto Sisters who paid £7,000 to the Trustees of the Institute and it became St Patrick's Primary School.

Loreto Convent

The Institute of the Blessed Virgin Mary was the first religious order to arrive in Bray. They had called their first private house in Dublin 'Loreto' in honour of the famous shrine of that name in Italy. They eventually became known world wide as the Loreto Sisters. The building, known as Sans Souci, where the convent now stands was owned by the Putlands who had lived there for fifty years. It stood in its own grounds of 78 acres, 100ft above sea level, commanding a magnificent view. The house was described as 'a chaste and elegant structure of the Tuscan order'. Beside the main house a conservatory was erected at a cost of £5,000. George Putland's motives for selling the property resulted from a family quarrel and he advised his solicitors to sell the estate. Mr Putland built an equally impressive mansion on another part of his estate that changed hands several times. The nuns opened a private boarding school in 1850 with seventy to ninety pupils, a secondary day school where all subjects were taught up to university entrance examination level. With a community of forty nuns, they expanded their activities rapidly and soon added a primary school for boys and girls.

Ravenswell Convent

At the invitation of Most Reverend Dr Donnelly, the parish priest, the Sodality of the Children of Mary came to Bray. In September 1896 they became established in Little Bray where they occupied the only available premises, known as 'Rack Rent House', on Dublin Road. The sisters were requested by the clergy to give religious instruction five days a week in Big and Little Bray schools and to prepare the pupils for the Sacraments. 'Rack Rent House' was used for infants during the day and for the instruction of converts in the evening. In April 1897 sixteen girls were consecrated Children of Mary. The Sodality of Christian Mothers was inaugurated in

March 1900 and, as the work continued to progress, the need for larger premises was recognised. In April 1901 Ravenswell was acquired by the Sisters, better known now as the Sisters of Charity. The people of the district turned up in the rain with a donkey and cart and a wheelbarrow to assist with the removal. They immediately set about converting the stables into schoolrooms, accommodating 300 pupils. The parish priest asked to be put at the disposal of the department of technical instruction and for some years classes in cookery, dressmaking and laundry were given every night by two qualified instructors with one of the Sisters in charge. These classes were later moved to the Little Flower Hall and ceased when the vocational school was established in the town. In 1918, when the town was struck by an influenza epidemic, the sisters made the school available to the people by converting it into a hospital and they assisted Doctor Raferty and the other doctors. Their efforts helped stem an escalation of the epidemic. Unfortunately a Sister from Saint Vincent's Hospital, who came to assist, fell ill and died. The school continued to expand and by 1930 there were 300 pupils on the roll book. Over the years several additional classrooms were added to the school, along with a new veranda. On 13 January 1937, the centenary of the canonisation of St Philomena, Pope Benedict XV officially and solemnly dedicated the school to her, as she was the special patron for the children of the working classes.

St Gerard's Preparatory School
Unique of its kind in Ireland, St Gerard's Preparatory School was founded entirely by lay management. It was established by an English convert, John James, in the famous house formerly known as Thornill in 1919. There was room for fifty boarders and as the prospectus said: 'with not very large numbers the school has the atmosphere of a large family rather than that usually associated with an institution.' There were good facilities for games – rugby, tennis, hockey and cricket – and they had their own open-air swimming pool. It still continues to flourish and now admits girls as well as boys. It has its own small private chapel with a resident chaplain appointed by the Archbishop of Dublin.

Colaiste Ciaran
Colaiste Ciaran was established in 1935 when the Irish Christian Brothers rented Old Connaught House and established there a house of studies where aspirants to the order were trained. All students were taught through the medium of Irish. The mansion, Classical in design with a Corinthian front, was somewhat austere in aspect, thought set in beautiful surround-ings.

Aravon

In 1862 Thomas Reginald Courtney, a classical scholar and gold medallist, opened a preparatory school for young Protestant boys at Fort View, one of the houses below the convent, on Sidmonton Road. He was joined in the venture by the Reverend Ormsby Handcock, curate of Bray. Four years later he took over the premises known as Aravon, on the Meath Road, and extended his scope to include older boys. The name 'Aravon' is obviously a reversal of 'Novara' and stood on land formerly belonging to Novara House. About this time Miss Haynes had a school for eight small boys in a terrace off the Quinsboro Road which she later transferred to premises near the Court House at the top of Bray Bridge and later still to Fort View. Between 1872 and 1892 Miss Haynes took over Aravon from Mr Courtenay and combined the two establishments. Originally it was called 'Bray School' with an 'Upper' House at Aravon and a 'Lower' House in Belgrave Terrace. She continued to run it with the assistance of various headmasters. The school's colours were black and gold and their motto was *Aspice Prospice Respice*. In 1894 it was taken over by Mr R.H. Bookey, under whose control many changes took place and numbers increased. Extensions were added including the famous dormitory known as the 'Hotel'. More attention was given to school sports, and the rugby team soon achieved the distinction of being one of the best school teams near Dublin. The school had a distinctly Anglo-Irish and military bias in the pre-First World War days, with many boys being sons of officers and a large number of them finding their way into the British Services. In a roll of honour of the dead of the First World War, forty-two masters and boys were shown as having lost their lives. That was a high percentage for a school whose maximum roll at any time was about ninety. In 1984 the entire school transferred to the old Conna Hill House.

French School

In 1864 Madame de Mailly founded the French School, a Protestant boarding school for young girls of all ages. It was located in three red-brick houses amalgamated into one at Sidmonton Place, consisting of thirty-two rooms and six bathrooms. Madame de Mailly was succeeded by Miss Williams and Miss Reilly as principals. A secret postal service between the boarders of the French School and the boys of Aravon flourished for some years. When the rector visited the French School he left his hat on the hall table and with great dexterity a girl would slip a note under the head-band. The hat would later be left in the hall when its wearer visited Aravon where an astute boy would extract the note and 'post' a return message in the same hiding place. The French School closed and was put up for auction on 18 July 1964. The building later housed the Forestry and Wildlife Services and is now an apartment block.

St Andrew's School

As early as 1866 the need for a Presbyterian school in Bray was felt but the plan did not immediately materialise. The idea was again mooted in 1887 when a site at the south side of the Methodist church was purchased and a special school fund was opened. After the Presbyterian community had contributed generously, a wider appeal was made among local residents. The foundation stone was laid by the Earl of Meath on 20 August 1887 and the school opened for pupils the following January. Mr Hilton was appointed as the first headmaster. As there was a considerable part of the cost still outstanding, the rector, Dr Irwin, at the suggestion of the congregation, went on a lecture tour to America and Canada. He brought back over £400 and the new school was declared free of debt that same year. The school was an immediate success and fulfilled a long-felt need in the growing community. In 1889 there were ninety-seven pupils on the register. In 1943 the building was completely destroyed by fire, caused by a fault in the wiring system. The building had been insured for £2,000 and although the new premises cost almost £4,000 the debt was completely cleared in two years. The school is now located on a new site at the base of Bray Head.

St Paul's Endowed School

St Paul's Endowed School, connected with the Church of Ireland, was situated on Herbert Road and was one of the most successful in the country.

Technical School

The population of the town increased from 6,888 in 1891 to 7,424 a decade later. At that time the larger employers were the railway repair works, the Municipal Electric Light Works and the building and tourist industries, but there was no formal institution to train young people for careers in these industries. In 1900 the Urban District Council proposed establishing a technical school to service these and other small industries in the area. The scheme was financed by a local contribution of a penny on the rates by the Urban District Council amounting to £120 per annum, and an annual grant from the Department of Agriculture and Technical Instruction of £400 per annum. Fees for classes provided additional revenue. Its objective was to offer a commercial and industrial education and a sound knowledge of the arts and crafts.

A lease was taken on the Infants' School at Brighton Terrace, where the school opened on 1 May 1902 and the first classes were conducted. Thomas Tomlinson was appointed first principal at a salary of £200. By the end of the first year, 217 pupils were studying a range of twenty subjects. Requests for courses in particular skills from Bray Laundry, Bray Cottage Industry, industries such as lacemaking (interested in design and drawing), hosiery, shirt-makers, beekeepers, railway workers, Bray Art Furniture Industry, (seeking help in upholstery) were all responded to. Within thirty years there was a need for a larger premises and a lease on a site on Florence Road was offered to the committee by the agents for the Quin estate for a term of 500 years at £10 per annum. Having overcome financial difficulties, the new school was built, consisting of thirteen rooms, at a cost of £5,783 and opened on 18 September 1933. A later extension provided woodwork facilities, an engineering room and gymnasium.

The unprecedented rate of increase in the population of Bray from 1965 onwards added to the needs for an extension and improved facilities for the VEC until finally in 1977 a site was acquired from the Loreto Order at a cost of £108,000. Saint Thomas's Community College, an impressive modern building catering for pupils up to Leaving Certificate standard, was opened on 18 March 1981, replacing the old school on Florence Road.

Elian's Spanish School

Ellian's Spanish School was founded in 1985 by Marisa Marin and Ignacio Monzonis. The school is located in Jubilee Hall, on Old Conna Road, 2 miles from Bray. The building has a long and illustrious history. In 1609, Richard Wingfield (later Lord Powerscourt) was granted the lands of Ferncullen by James I and built the castle to celebrate the reign of the king. The building consisted of three elegant reception rooms, five large bedchambers and a fine garden and coach house.

From the beginning of the nineteenth century many people rented Jubilee Hall from Lord Powerscourt. The most famous guest was Daniel O'Connell who stayed there regularly with his son. The land and castle remained in the hands of Lord Powerscourt until 1930 when he lost it in a game of cards with the King of England. A third card player, a Mr Dogherty, advanced a small sum of money to Powerscourt and in return he handed over the castle so that he could continue playing. That was the end of the Powerscourt family connection with Jubilee Hall.

15

LITERARY CONNECTIONS

James Joyce

Bray has always been a magnet for creative talent and many distinguished writers have had connections with the town.

One of the most famous Bray residents of all time must surely be James Joyce. Joyce's first memories, which open *Portrait of the Artist as a Young Man* and give an account of his youth, were not of Brighton Square, Dublin, where he was born but of a house beside the sea in Bray. His father's desire to live near water and far from his wife's relations were the main reasons for moving his family to the seaside resort. In May 1887 he took them to live at No.1 Martello Terrace, a fashionable three-storey residence so close to the sea that the area in front of their house was frequently flooded by high tides. His wife shared his love of music and for a time they sang in the choir in Little Bray Church.

James' brother Stanislaus wrote a book of reminiscences of the family entitled *My Brother's Keeper* in which he recalled memories of many events in Bray. On Sundays John Joyce invited friends to spend the day at his home. After lunch they would enjoy a stroll around the Cliff Walk, return for dinner and sing and drink all evening in the drawing-room on the first floor accompanied by Mrs Joyce on the piano. Two frequent guests were Alfred Bergan, later to become assistant to the sub-sheriff of Dublin, and Tom Devlin. Of these parties James Joyce wrote to Bergan in 1934: 'We used to have merry evenings in our house, used we not?'

It was perhaps the prospect of living in such a healthy resort that brought so many of Joyce Snr's relative to stay with them. There was his Uncle William O'Connell from Cork, and John Kelly from Tralee who appeared in *Portrait of the Artist as a Young Man*, under the name of John Casey. Kelly was imprisoned several times for Land League agitation and one evening a constable, also named Joyce, a friend of the family, came to the house to warn him that he would have to issue a warrant for Kelly the next morning. Kelly escaped by car that night.

Soon after the Joyces moved to Bray they were joined by Mrs 'Dante' Hearn Conway from Cork, who was the governess for the children. She was too embittered by a disastrous marriage to blend easily into the tolerant, high-spirited household. Quite early in his life Joyce learned to fear religion, a strong theme in much of his later writing. His fear of dogs and preference for cats dated from the time when he badly bitten by an excited Irish terrier while he and Stanislaus were throwing stones into the sea near the Baths.

James Vance, who ran the chemist's shop in Main Street and Albert Walk, lived in No.4 Martello Terrace. He was a hard-working man, whose wife suffered from heart disease and spent most of the day resting and reading novels. Their daughter Eileen and James Joyce both attended a kindergarten run by a Miss Raynor in Bray and the two were always paired off together. The town was full of young girls, those 'seaside girls' that remained in his memory for many years to surface again in *Ulysses*. Could his love of resorts in later life have arisen from his early memories of Bray?

James' voice was good enough for him to join his parents in singing at an amateur concert at the Bray Boat Club on 26 June 1888, when he was only six years old. He was an adventurous child and at the age of seven he rode his tricycle from the outskirts of Dublin to Bray to visit a nurse while his distraught parents searched for him amongst their friends and family. John Joyce had a high opinion of his eldest son and, determined to give him the best education in Ireland, sent him to Clongowes Wood College. On 1 September 1888 James became a boarder at the college but he always looked forward to his visits home where his family received him warmly. In 1891 John Joyce's financial problems increased and they had to leave Bray and withdraw James from Clongowes in June of that year.

The house in Martello Terrace was the setting for the famous Christmas dinner scene in *Portrait of the Artist as a Young Man*, when the father and John Kelly argue over Parnell's betrayal and death and the infuriated Dante leaves the table.

An inaccuracy occurs in *Ulysses* with reference to Bray. It reads: 'They halted, looking towards the blunt cape of Bray Head that lay on the water like the snout of a sleeping whale.' The location for this observation was the top of Sandycove Martello Tower but this is impossible as the headland of Dalkey blocks the view of Bray. Even Molly Bloom, in her soliloquy, mentions Bray as she prepares for a picnic: 'I'd never again in this life get in a boat with him after him at Bray telling the boatman he knew how to row.'

James Joyce was never again to visit Bray but in 1935 his daughter Lucia, who was introvert and spent long spells in asylums, accompanied his sister Eileen to her home in the town.

Oscar Wilde

Another famous and controversial literary figure, Oscar Wilde, had connections with Bray. His father Sir William Wilde, a prominent surgeon, built five high-class residences, Nos 1–4 Esplanade Terrace and Elsinore (which is now the Strand Hotel) on the seafront. When Sir William was knighted in 1864 the family was socially and financially secure, but he was to become involved in a scandal that same year. He had affairs with various women and one of them, a patient of his, Mary Travers, was not discreet about their relationship. She was an attractive nineteen-year-old when she went to Dr Wilde in Dublin for treatment of an inflamed ear but he took more than a professional interest in her. When he grew tired and wanted to break off the affair, Mary began sending a series of anonymous letters to his wife describing him as a spiteful old lunatic. She claimed that he interfered with her and produced a pamphlet to ensure that her allegations became widely known. It described the rape of one 'Florence Boyle Price' by a 'Doctor Quilp' and left no doubt as to Quilp's true identity. His wife took the children, Willie, Oscar and Isola, out to Esplanade Terrace to avoid the scandal. Miss Travers followed her to Bray and sent small boys selling the pamphlet to her door. Growing impatient, Lady Wilde wrote an angry letter to Mary's father, Dr Travers, who was Professor of Medical Jurisprudence at Trinity College Dublin, complaining of his daughter's actions.

Miss Travers accidentally came across the letter in her father's papers and some weeks later she sued Lady Wilde for libel. She claimed £2,000 damages, knowing that Sir William would be cited as co-defendant since by the Irish laws of the time he was legally responsible for the actions of his wife. The jury took two hours to make their decision and brought in a verdict for the plaintiff, assessing the damages at one farthing. The publicity given to the case had an unfortunate effect on Sir William who rapidly deteriorated. He died in the spring of 1876 when twenty-two-year-old Oscar was in his second year in Oxford. Oscar was left the property in Bray but due to his father's complex financial affairs he was forced to sell the houses. He received less than £3,000 on the sale, most of which he lost in lawsuits, confused contracts and too many agents.

Sir Walter Scott

In July 1825, while Sir Walter Scott was working on his extensive biography of Napoleon, he made an excursion to Ireland with his son-and-law and biographer, John Gibson Lockhart, and his unmarried daughter Anne. They visited many parts of the country and during their excursions to Wicklow, Scott was the guest of Mr (afterwards Sir Philip) Crampton, an eminent surgeon, and of Lord Plunket, the lawyer and orator at Old Connaught. Scott was impressed by the acute logic and brilliant eloquence of Plunket. Plunket accompanied Scott on his visit to Glendalough in which the poet

inscribed his name on Saint Kevin's Bed. In a letter to the novelist Maria
Edgeworth, dated 27 July, Scott himself described his visit to Wicklow:

I am just returned from Wicklow delighted with all I have seen. The mere wood,
water and wilderness have not so much the charm of novelty for a North as for a
South Briton. But these are intermingled with an appearance of fertility which
never accompanies them in our land, and with a brilliancy of verdure which
justifies your favourite epithet of the Green Isle.

Lockhart wrote to his wife a description of a tour in County Wicklow:
'Down the valley to Powerscourt, a grand domain, with very grand trees.
The Dargle, a superior even to its fame – an indiscriminately beautiful
mixture of wood, water, rocks, hills, valley…'

During his visit Scott enjoyed sumptuous dinners in Old Connaught and
leisurely strolls with Plunket along the banks of the Dargle. Frequently he
sat meditating beneath the big tree at the junction of Old Connaught,
writing and smoking his pipe. Later Scott was to record favourable
comments of his trip to Bray in his journal.

Sir Arthur Conan Doyle

Sir Arthur Conan Doyle, the creator of Sherlock Holmes, stayed for a short
while in Rahan House on Killarney Road to gather photographic
evidence for his theory on psychic phenomena. After so many deaths in the
First World War, Conan Doyle was convinced that life must exist after death
and thereafter spiritualism was to occupy the major part of his energies. He
even discovered an ability to act as a medium for trance writing. Most of
his work, both literary and photographic, was undertaken in a glasshouse at
the rear of the house. The fruits of his visit to Bray and other centres was
a book entitled *The Coming of the Fairies*; the ridicule with which this was
greeted greatly distressed him.

Lennox Robinson

Following the production of his play *The Clancy Name*, Lennox Robinson
spent several weeks in Bray either going to the Abbey or sitting on the
esplanade writing the second and least successful of all his dramas *The Cross
Roads*. As a younger man Robinson had gone out with a girl from
Duncairn Terrace in Bray but her family objected and he terminated the
relationship.

Philip Rooney

Philip Rooney first came to Bray in 1942 as a bank official with the
Hibernian Bank. Two years later, owing to ill health he was forced to retire
from the bank and took up writing full-time. During his period in Bray he

wrote, and had published, four novels: *North Road*, *The Long Day*, *The Golden Coast* and his best known work, *Captain Boycott*. The last-named, published in 1946, told of the notorious Mayo landlord and the rise of his tenants against tyranny, and proved a huge success. Two Cities Films bought the film rights and it was filmed in Ireland with Stewart Granger in the leading role. Rooney was actively involved with the Bray Literary and Debating Society and served several terms as president of the society. In 1950 he joined Radio Éireann's drama department as a script writer and remained in that position until 1961 when the television service was introduced and he was appointed chief script editor. Philip Rooney, a quiet, unassuming man, lived with his family until his death in March 1962.

Liam O'Flaherty

In the late 1920s when his literary output was running at a high level, Liam O'Flaherty, the famed author of *The Informer*, grew restless and was constantly on the move. He found seclusion in a house on Seapoint Road for a time before moving to London, France and even Russia.

Other Writers

One of the country's foremost short story writers, Mary Lavin had an abiding love for Bray, having spent many childhood holidays in the Bray Head Hotel. The novelist, Jennifer Johnston also has fond memories of the town and recalled reminiscences her grandmother told her about the resort at the turn of the century. 'She stayed with her family in the Bray Head Hotel every summer and enjoyed swimming and the sophistication and glamour of strolling along the promenade.'

Richard Power who wrote the powerful novel *The Hungry Grass*, a study of loneliness, lived in Bray and died there aged forty-two on 12 February 1970.

Some noted writers have set their material in Bray. Sean O'Faolain's short story *An Inside Outside Complex* was set in the resort, out of season. The town was also the focal point of James Plunkett's short story *The Half-Crown*. Several of the Bray-born playwright James Douglas's radio and television plays were set in the town. It has also featured in the film and written work of Neil Jordan and a novel by Leyland Bardwell.

The roll books of Aravon school contains the names of many boys who were later to gain prominence in their respective fields including H. Le Fanu, who became Archbishop of Australia; Hugh Rigley, who became surgeon to King George V; and Dr William Collis, who played rugby for Ireland. Collis wrote his autobiography *The Silver Fleece* and later several plays based on his experiences as a doctor working with the under-privileged in Dublin. The eminent Irish author, Monk Gibbon, was a teacher in Aravon for a period.

Michael Le Fanu of the famous literary family, who became an admiral in the Royal Navy, had childhood connections with Bray. He attended Aravon and spent the holidays with his Uncle Tom who lived in Abington. His father was the chief coastguard officer for south-east Ireland and was based at the naval base in Kingstown.

The most distinguished former pupils of Aravon were Roger Casement, who attended the school in 1875, and John Millington Synge, who had to make his way there every day by train from his home in Orwell Park in Rathgar. He was a popular boy and particularly enjoyed swimming in Naylor's Cove with his classmates. From 1880 his family took their holidays in various places in County Wicklow, including Bray. In the area Synge turned his attention to the people of the countryside and he enjoyed their company. On the road he would stop and chat with tramps and record their stories and unusual phrases in his notebook. Synge lived among the country people in Wicklow and the Aran Islands and used what he observed to write *The Playboy of the Western World*.

Many of the Le Fanu family lived in and around Bray during the mid-1800s. The noted novelist, Joseph Sheridan Le Fanu, who made his reputation with novels of mystery and the supernatural, in his *An Authentic Narrative of a Haunted House*, published in 1862, described a summer resort to which the narrator and his wife retired as invalids. He had spent various prolonged periods in Bray. During the time he was writing *Uncle Silas* he was also absorbed in his own family history and was struck by illness. From late April until the first week of June 1864 he had been the victim of influenza followed by bronchitis, and he had spent much of the six or seven weeks at 11 Brennan's Terrace, a temporary retreat from Dublin. He died in 1873.

W.R. Le Fanu, Sheridan's younger brother, lived at Summerhill, Enniskerry. He wrote *Seventy Years of Irish Life*, a book full of anecdotes and reminiscences in which Bray and the Dargle are mentioned several times. Ravenswell, one of the larger mansions in the parish, was built overlooking the Dargle estuary. An impressive list of people lived at Ravenswell, including Isaac Weld who bought it in 1813. Weld was not a wealthy man although he wrote several volumes of his travels abroad that were translated into many languages. He was a man of great culture and both he and his wife were popular in the district for the forty years they lived there. He died in Ravenswell in August 1856.

Many distinguished people lived in Saint Valerie's, a picturesque location near the Dargle Bridge. In residence in 1810 was W. Cooper Walker, an author whose most notable publication was *Historical Memories on Italian Tragedy*. He carried on a correspondence with some of the most eminent literary men of the age in various parts of the world.

Shanganagh Castle was the home of General George Cockburn, an eccentric and wealthy man who was born in Dublin in 1763. Cockburn joined the Grenadier Guards and acted as aide-de-camp at the siege of Gibraltar. He studied on the continent and served in Sicily during the Napoleonic Wars. On his return to Shanganagh Castle, which he extended in 1818, he published two books covering his travels. He was promoted to general in 1821. He also served as a magistrate for Wicklow and Dublin.

William Cobbett, while visiting Cockburn at Shanganagh in 1834, completed his book *Legacy of Labourers*. Other guests included Harold Nicolson, the husband of Vita Sackville-West. When Cockburn died on 18 August 1847 he was the fourth general in seniority in the British Army.

Since 1969 many foreign writers have taken up residence in County Wicklow to avail themselves of the tax-free exemption from their writing income. One of these, best-selling thriller writer, Alistair MacLean, maintained a low profile for the duration of his stay in Bray during the late 1970s. MacLean, the author of such successful books as *The Guns of Navarone* and *When Eight Bells Toll*, lived in the secluded Violet Hill at the top of the Herbert Road. He left Bray in 1979 to live in Switzerland.

Much more conspicuous was another best-selling author, Frederick Forsyth, who lived at the same period in Kilgarron House. Forsythe, the author of *The Day of the Jackal* and *The Odessa File* completed his fourth highly successful novel, *The Devil's Alternative*, during his years in Enniskerry. He also wrote the screenplay for the film *Cry of the Innocent*. In 1981 he returned to England.

Several clerical writers have had associations with Bray. Father J.A. Gaughan, the Listowel-born historian and biographer of Tom O'Donnell, the O'Rahilly and Austin Stack, served as chaplain to Presentation College from 1957. During this period Father Gaughan also played full-back for Bray Emmets GAA football club.

The Dublin born playwright Father Desmond Forristal, who had several plays successfully staged including *Black Man's Country*, *The Horrid Popish Plot* and *Kolbe*, served a number of years as a curate in the Most Holy Redeemer Church in the 1970s until he was transferred to Iona Road, Glasnevin. His love for the arts was evident by his encouragement of local drama and musical groups.

Bray and its environs still maintain their attraction for creative people and is now home for Clare Boylan, Lee Dunne, James Douglas, Cathy Kelly, Cormac MacRaoise, Grace Wynn Jones, Tomas MacAnna, Wesley Burrows, Peter Regan, Donal O'Donovan, Daithi Ó hOgain, Mary Rose Callaghan and Diarmuid Breathnach. The musician and composer Phil Coulter and the singer Mary Coughlan are presently Bray residents.

16

FAMOUS RESIDENTS
AND VISITORS

After the death of Isaac Weld in 1856 Doctor Richard O'Reilly Dease
came to Ravenswell. He was accompanied by his infamous wife, Anna
Maria, and their son Matthew who was a doctor of law and one-time MP
for Louth. Matthew was somewhat eccentric and refused to reside in
Ravenswell; instead he lived in a humble cottage elsewhere in the town.
Mrs O'Reilly Dease preferred to sleep in a yacht in the bay although she
was prone to seasickness. She said that 'life spent with a bowl under your
nose was preferable to living in Bray'. She admired a local curate, Father
James Healy, and felt that he should be of higher rank. She sent for Cardinal
Cullen and on his arrival in Ravenswell she demanded that Father Healy
be made a parish priest. Soon afterwards Father Healy was promoted to
parish priest but Mrs O'Reilly Dease was still unhappy, believing that Little
Bray was beneath his station. In 1894 he was transferred to Ballybrack.
Father Healy only survived his transfer for ten months and was buried in
Glasnevin.

Whilst Father Healy was curate in Bray he lived above Miss Barry's cake
shop and on his appointment as parish priest of Little Bray he moved to
one of the two houses later known as the Meath Convalescent Home. He
was to become famous for his dinner parties, at which the food was plain
but the conversation stimulating. Amongst his eminent guests were judges,
novelists, poets, noblemen and royalty. Judge William Keogh and Judge
James Lawson were among Father Healy's most intimate friends and during
the Fenian period, when their lives were in danger, they would often call
to consult him.

Father Healy's love of Protestants, as warm as for his own flock, earned
him the reputation of 'the Protestant Priest'. The prince of Saxe-Weimar
had been commander of the king's forces in Ireland for some time when
he made the acquaintance of Father Healy. The prince, at a dinner in

Dublin Castle not knowing that Father Healy was in earshot, remarked that he had heard that real Wicklow mutton with gravy on it could only be found at one table – that of the Roman Catholic priest of Little Bray. As a result a cheerful voice was heard to say, addressing the prince's aide-de-camp, 'If His Serene Highness would be good enough to visit my hermitage, I promise to show him not only the mutton but the gravy too.' The informal invitation was accepted on the spot and the prince dined with Father Healy in Little Bray.

Among the people who resided in Saint Valerie's were members of the judiciary, including Justice John Crampton, one of the judges who tried and sentenced Daniel O'Connell to imprisonment in 1844. As an elderly man he married the young daughter of Michael William Balfe, composer of *The Bohemian Girl*.

Daniel O'Connell paid many visits to Bray to address meetings, attend social functions and stay overnight in Jubilee Hall. One of his most prestigious visits was when the township commissioners and clergy played host to him at a public breakfast in Quin's Hotel at which the town's leaders of industry and commerce were introduced to him. During his stay the street was crowded to excess and the area in front of the hotel was impassable. Mr Putland intended joining the party but was prevented by illness. He gave his workers the day off and allowed them to cut down his shrubbery to decorate the Main Street as a tribute to the Liberator. A band, which played popular and patriotic airs outside the hotel, was driven in cars in front of O'Connell when he left at 9.45 a.m. amid the enthusiastic acclamation of thousands.

Some of the judiciary who lived in Bray were quite eccentric. Judge William Keogh went insane as a result of VD and was sent to an asylum at Bingen-on-Rhine where he attacked his valet and later cut his own throat.

Judge Le Fry, a chief justice of Ireland, lived in Ardmore House and even in his nineties still sat on the bench and refused to step down. During a murder trial he slept a good deal and when the accused was found guilty he was unsure of the wording of the pronouncement and the prosecution council had to prompt him. Another murder trial was planted on him in which he took no notes and it consequently forced his retirement.

Judge James Lawson who lived in a house beside Hollywood, vehemently condemned the Invincibles and imprisoned many of their members. A young Invincible named Delaney was sent to assassinate him but the attempt failed and he was arrested.

In the early 1860s Sir Robert Stewart came to live at Hollybrook and soon afterwards formed the Bray Philharmonic Society, with himself as president and conductor. They first met in a house on Quinsboro Road but the rooms were too small and Sir Robert lent his own fine drawing-room for the meetings, where many delightful evenings were spent. Under his baton Bray, for the first time, heard the *Messiah, Judas Maccabaeus* and *Acis and Galatea*. Sir Robert was a patient teacher in spite of his highly-strung temperament. He was endowed with extraordinary technical musical ability and was organist in Christ Church and Saint Patrick's Cathedral in Dublin and also Christ Church in Bray. He died in 1894.

Another distinguished figure associated with Christ Church, Bray, was Sir Herbert Hamilton Harty. He was born in Hillsborough, County Down, in 1879 into a musical environment. His father taught him the piano and viola, and when he was only twelve he became organist at a church in County Antrim. Later he moved to Belfast and Dublin. His first appointment on graduating was as organist in Christ Church, Bray. He remained in that position for six years and lived at Clara, Herbert Road. At the same time he was composing and winning prizes for chamber works. His works included *Comedy Overture, The Mystic Trumpeter* and an arrangement of Irish folk-tunes. The highlight of the versatile Hamilton Harty's career was when he became conductor of the Hallé Orchestra, Manchester, in 1920. He was a controversial figure and strongly objected to women playing in the orchestra. Sir Hamilton Harty remained with the Hallé until 1933. He died in Brighton in 1941.

Paul Henry, a Belfast-born artist, came to live in Bray in 1945 having lost his sight. He lived in many houses in the area, including No. 1 Sidmonton Square. He died on 24 August 1958 and is buried in Saint Patrick's graveyard, Enniskerry.

In political terms Bray has produced some outstanding figures, most notably Cearbhall Ó Dalaigh, who became Chief Justice in 1961, having been a judge of the Supreme Court and Attorney General. In 1974 he was inaugurated as the fifth president of Ireland. He was born on 12 February 1911 at No.85 Main Street, the second son of a fish and poultry shop manager, Richard Daly, and his wife Una. His mother had been active in the nationalist movement and Cearbhall and his brother Aenghus remembered her brother Joe Thornton coming to their home after the 1916 Rising and his subsequent arrest there by the RIC. In 1915 Cearbhall was enrolled at the Loreto Convent but the Mother Superior saw fit to have his mother withdraw him after only one day. Three years later he was a pupil at Big Bray's National School, Herbert Road. He was also proud of his association with Bray's oldest educational establishment. The family lived for a while at No.3 Old Court Terrace, Vevay Road, which was then on the edge of the town. When Cearbhall was thirteen years old his father died and they moved to live in Dublin. His aunt, Mary Thornton worked in the post office in Bray and she provided the money for the two boys to attend the Ring Gaeltacht in County Waterford.

The town of his birth was to honour Cearbhall Ó Dalaigh when, as president, he received a civic reception on 21 September 1975. Ó Dalaigh was a judge at the European Court of Justice in Luxembourg when he was nominated by the three main political parties as an agreed candidate for the presidency, in 1974. When he referred two bills of the Coalition government (the Criminal Law Jurisdiction Bill and the Emergency Powers Bill) to the Supreme Court he was denounced as 'a thundering disgrace' by the then minister for defence, Patrick Donegan. When no disciplinary action was taken by the Taoiseach, Liam Cosgrave, President Ó Dalaigh resigned on 22 October 1976. He died the following year and was buried at Tahilla, near Sneem in County Kerry.

Desmond FitzGerald, who became a prominent politician, lived in Bray for many years from 1915. He died on 9 April 1947. (His career is documented in Chapter 10.) One of his children, Garret, was to follow his father's example and entered politics. Garret spent his childhood, from the age of two to eleven, in Bray, at Fairy Hill House, a large house on Killarney Road, which consisted of three acres of gardens and thirteen acres of farmland. Young Garret attended Saint Brigid's School on Quinsboro Road where for a time he was the only boy in a class of girls. The constant flow of distinguished visitors to their home made a lasting impression on him – W.B. Yeats, Jacques Maritain, T.S. Eliot, Ernest Blythe, Sean McEntee and Lord Longford. In March 1937 they had to sell the house and leave Bray. Garret went on to distinguish himself as an economist, government minister and finally reached the pinnacle of a highly successful career on becoming Taoiseach.

Other government ministers born in Bray are Gemma Hussey and Michael Woods, both of whom served in a number of ministries. In more recent times Liz McManus and Dick Roche served as junior ministers.

17

FILM-MAKING IN BRAY

Over forty years before the opening of Ardmore Studios, Bray was already playing an important part in early film production. A local man, Billy Power, who had returned from Manchester with the intention of making films, was the leading figure in the venture. He planned to meet the demand existing for moving pictures. Power ran a barber's shop on Novara Road which was as much a film studio and laboratory as it was a hairdressers. In 1917 he set up the Bray Musical and Dramatic Society for the purpose of using it as a recruiting ground for his films. The following year he wrote, produced and directed a short comedy with the intriguing title *Willie Scouts while Jessie Pouts*. He was pleased with the results and received such support locally that he founded the Celtic Film Company.

Power's second project was a more ambitious two-hour film *Rosaleen Dhu*, the story of a Fenian who had to leave Ireland and joined the French Foreign Legion. The film was shot around Bray with the beach at Arklow used for desert scenes. Those early silent films were shot by a camera in a fixed position but Power invested in a camera capable of panning, for the sum of £88. His cameraman was Matt Tobin, the blind church organist. No expense was sparred on the camera but the props and cast cost nothing. The film was processed in wooden barrels at the rear of the barber's shop. Encouraged by the success, the company planned their second feature, *An Irish Vendetta*, with Billy Power in the main role. They were filming the story's climax on Leopardstown Race Course on 6 June 1920 when tragedy struck. Power's horse bolted, throwing him onto the railings. He died two days later in hospital and the film was never completed. In 1932 the last print of *Rosaleen Dhu* was destroyed by the floods in Little Bray.

In the 1940s film production in Europe was greatly hampered by the war, but neutral Ireland offered facilities not readily available elsewhere. Extensive exterior filming was virtually impossible in Britain and France.

In 1943 Laurence Olivier chose Powerscourt estate to film the Battle of Agincourt for his production of *Henry V*. To swell the action scenes 510 infantry and 164 horsemen were recruited. The horsemen were mainly unemployed and members of the LDF (Local Defence Force) from nearby counties. Horsemen were paid £1 per day. The setting resembled an enormous army camp with the extras living in tents. Chain mail was knitted from wool by girls from the Institute for the Blind. The actual Battle of Agincourt segment deservedly belongs with the great sequences of cinema history.

Scenes for many other films have been shot in Powerscourt, including *Moby Dick* with Gregory Peck, *Captain Lightfoot* with Rock Hudson, *Darling Lili* with Julie Andrews, *The Blue Max* with George Peppard, *Ella Enchanted* with Anne Hathaway and *Moll Flanders* with Robin Wright.

In 1958 Ireland got its own film studios. In May that year Ardmore Studios in Bray was officially opened by the Minister for Industry and Commerce, Sean Lemass. The studio was a completely self-contained film centre, capable of handling productions of any size or character. The studio got off to an encouraging start with a series of filmed Abbey plays beginning with *Home is the Hero* by Walter Macken, with Macken himself in the title role.

Shake Hands with the Devil, directed by Michael Anderson, was the first major production to be shot in Ardmore. The film, set in Dublin in 1921, starred James Cagney, Don Murray, Dana Wynter and Sybil Thorndike. *A Terrible Beauty*, the next major film to go before the cameras in Ardmore, starred Robert Mitchum and Richard Harris. The setting was a border town during the IRA campaign of the 1940s. The early 1960s saw a continuous flow of medium budget films – *The Siege of Sidney Street*, *Johnny Nobody* and *The Webster Boy*. A controversial film, *The Mark*, brought a badly needed boost to Ardmore. Stuart Whitman starred as a man trying to re-establish himself in society after a prison sentence for child abuse, and was the first Ardmore actor to receive an Oscar nomination.

Term of Trial, the next large-scale film to go into production, was a tense drama set in an English school and starred Laurence Olivier and Sarah Miles. A market scene was shot on Bray's Quinsboro Road. In 1964 *The Spy who came in from the Cold* was directed at Ardmore by Martin Ritt and starred Richard Burton and Claire Bloom. Burton received an Oscar nomination for his role as a seedy spy. For *The Blue Max*, areas of County Wicklow were skilfully transformed to recreate the Battle of the Somme. The producers employed several hundred Irish troops to play Irish soldiers. Fighter planes staged dog fights over the county. The film starred George Peppard, Ursula Andress and James Mason.

The American director John Huston, who did much to foster an Irish film industry, directed three films in County Wicklow – *The List of Adrian*

Messanger, Sinful Davey and *The Mackintosh Man.* The actor Laurence Harvey starred in two films in Bray in the 1960s – *The Running Man*, with location scenes in Christ Church and on the seafront, and *Of Human Bondage*, with Kim Novak, including a funeral scene on Seapoint Road. The Harbour Bar has featured in many films, including *The Quare Fellow* and *Brotherly Love* with Peter O'Toole.

Other important films to be produced in Ardmore during this period were *The First Great Train Robbery* with Sean Connery, *Images* directed by Robert Altman, *The Purple Taxi* starring Fred Astaire and *Da* with Martin Sheen. John Boorman, a good friend to Ardmore, choose the studio when making *Zardoz*, a futuristic film starring Sean Connery. Some years later Boorman directed *Excalibur* in Ardmore with Nicol Williamson, Helen Mirren, Liam Neeson and Gabriel Byrne. Another renowned director, Stanley Kubrick, filmed *Barry Lyndon* in Powerscourt and other stately homes.

In 1981 Neil Jordan wrote and directed his first feature film, *Angel*, which he partly shot on location in Bray. In 1990 Jordan returned to direct *The Miracle*, which was set and filmed entirely in Bray. The drama starring Donal McCann and Beverley D'Angelo gave much enjoyment and employment during the summer months. In 1995 Neil Jordan took over the Carlisle Grounds in Bray for the dramatic 1920 Bloody Sunday sequence of *Michael Collins*. An appeal went out for 5,000 extras to appear for free as spectators at the match and the result was a spectacular re-enactment of the bloody event. *Michael Collins*, starring Liam Neeson and Julia Roberts, became the most popular film in Ireland and broke box-office records. A section of Jordan's next film, *The Butcher Boy*, based on the best selling novel by Pat McCabe, was filmed at Ardmore Studios and on location. The film starred Stephen Rea and Fiona Shaw.

Many of the elaborate scenes for *Braveheart* were filmed at Ardmore Studios. Mel Gibson directed and starred in the film which was shot in a variety of Irish locations including the Sally Gap area where one of the bloody battle scenes were staged. 1,500 members of the defence forces played English soldiers and Scots. The film won five Oscars including Best Film and Best Director.

Over the years Bray town and its environs have provided locations for many major films. *My Left Foot*, Jim Sheridan's directorial debut was filmed in Killruddery House and Connolly Square. In the film, Daniel Day Lewis played the disabled writer Christy Brown and recalled his amazing rise to fame. Day Lewis and Brenda Fricker won Oscars for their outstanding performances in the film.

In 1991 Tom Cruise, Nicole Kidman and director Ron Howard came to Killruddery House to shoot sequences for the adventure film, *Far and Away*. Director Mike Newell shot several scenes for the successful *Into the West* around Bray. Newell returned to Bray to stage a mock football match in the Carlisle Grounds for *An Awfully Big Adventure* with Alan Rickman and Hugh Grant. The wedding at the beginning of *The Commitments*, based on Roddy Doyle's best-selling book, was shot in the Bray Head Hotel. The hotel was also a location for *Gold in the Street*, *Bloody Sunday* and *Laws of Attraction*.

In 1997 John Boorman returned to Bray for his controversial film, *The General*, based on the life of the Dublin criminal, Martin Cahill. Scenes for the film were shot on the seafront, on Quinsboro Road and in a house on the Herbert Road. Brendan Gleeson took the leading role. Anjelica Huston took over the promenade for a sequence in Agnes Brown.

One of the beneficiaries of the huge increase in film-making in Ireland in the 1990s was Ardmore Studios. Many major films and television series have utilised the studio including *Kidnapped*, *The Family*, *The Old Curiosity Shop*, *Jake's Progress*, *Sweeney Todd*, *Evelyn* and *Oliver Twist*. Large exterior London street sets have been constructed on the studio lot.

In recent years scenes for television series have been filmed in Bray. Many streets and buildings turned up in the popular RTE series *Glenroe*. The successful BBC series *Ballykissangel* featured several Bray exteriors during the run of the series. Sequences for the BBC series *The Ambassador*, starring Pauline Collins as the British Ambassador in Ireland, were shot on the seafront.

It is not surprising, with this volume of film activity in Bray, that the town should produce its own film-makers. Two Bray film-makers, Paddy Breathnach and Morgan O'Sullivan have distinguished themselves within the industry. Breathnach has directed *Ailsa*, *I Went Down*, *Blow Dry* and *Man About Dog*. O'Sullivan has been co-producer of a series of successful projects filmed in Ireland including *Scarlett*, *Braveheart*, *Count of Monte Cristo*, *Reign of Fire* and *King Arthur*.

18

THE TOWN TODAY

Although Bray, with the exception of half a mile of greenery at Crinken, is almost an extension of Dublin, at heart it remains a provincial town. Every Saturday afternoon, the town swells in size with the influx of shoppers from the environs of Shankill, Enniskerry, Kilmacanogue and Greystones. There are excellent shopping facilities in the area, with modern shopping centres and branches of the national multiples.

Today Bray is primarily a staging post for brief visits or a dormitory town for commuters to the city. The once close-knit community, where sons and daughters took over family businesses, has been augmented by such an invasion of newcomers to the new housing estates that there has been a remarkable increase in the population since 1961. In the Census of 1971 the population of Bray stood at 15,737. By 1981 this had increased to 22,853, an increase of 46 per cent. In 1986 the population had increased further to 24,870. Today the population of the Urban District of Bray is 26,216. The cosmopolitan newcomers have formed amicable relations with the deep-rooted locals, cautious at first to offer the welcoming hand. Fortunately unemployment has dipped, mainly due to the opening of new outlets in the industrial estates, and to the building boom.

Products produced in the town include biscuits, toothpaste, computers, cardboard packaging, printing, windows, nylon and bulbs. Industrial sites on the Boghall Road, Southern Cross Road and Dublin Road now accommodate many small industries. In the 1970s and '80s many firms specialising in printing and computer related products were established in Bray. There was widespread concern when the Nixdorf plant closed but it has since been replaced by the highly successful Dell Computer Company that employs 450 people. The extent of the growth has only marginally affected the many natural amenities of parks and woodlands. A section of Killruddery estate was sold for road improvement and housing.

Accommodation currently on offer extends from one-bedroom apartments to luxury demesnes.

There has been considerable upgrading of the road system with the Shankill and Bray bypass saving valuable time on journeys from Dublin southwards. In 1995 the Southern Cross route opened to provide a connection from the Bray–Greystones road to the N11. In 2003 the lengthy roads works on the Kilmacanogue–Glen of the Downs road were finally completed and pressure was relieved on traffic commuting to and from the city. The town is also serviced by the DART (Dublin Area Rapid Transit) that links Bray with Dun Laoghaire, Dublin and Howth. In 1988 another major project assisted by European funding was the Bray Sewerage Scheme which takes sewerage 2.4km off shore and features state-of-the-art building close to the harbour. For the past century the promenade has been under constant threat from the sea with flooding causing serious structural problems. In a coastal protection scheme tons of rocks and shingle were placed along the seashore protecting the promenade from pounding waves.

Bray, only 12 miles from Dublin, has become a prime real estate location and a commuter base for many couples working in the capital. Following the completion of the River Dargle Flood Relief Scheme, several housing estates were built adjoining the river. The old Maltings site was cleared and an attractive range of apartments and houses has been constructed. At Seapoint Road, another housing estate was built, close to the river. Many new housing estates have been developed in the vicinity of the Southern Cross route including Ridelsford, Belmont, Oakglen, Earlscroft, Hollybrook and Swanbrook. North of the river Corke Abbey and Old Conna Woods were constructed.

In recent years Bray has begun to recapture some of its former glory and prestige and regain its position as one of Ireland's premier resorts. Many British and European coach tours are based in Bray hotels for tours of the Garden of Ireland. Many business premises have had overdue facelifts, bringing back an air of elegance to the seafront. There is more pride in the appearance of shop fronts with the almost total elimination of plastic signs. The revival has been spearheaded by the energetic Bray and District Chamber of Commerce and the Beautiful Bray Association.

Bray is renowned for its many cultural events and organisations. These include Signal Arts Centre, Bray Arts Club, Bray Musical Society, Bray Concert Band, Bray One-Act Drama Festival, Square One Theatre Group, Dry Choral Society and Conradh na Gaeilge. In 2002 the Mermaid Arts Centre was opened in Bray and provided the town with its first purpose-built municipal arts centre offering concerts, plays, films and art exhibitions.

There are a wide range of sporting activities and clubs based in Bray including Bray Emmets, Bray Wanderers, Bray Bowling Club, Clay Pigeon Club, Bray Strollers and County Wicklow Lawn Tennis Club. There are

several golf clubs within the environs of the town, including Bray Golf
Club, Woodbrook, Old Conna Golf Club and Bray Head Par 3. Bray
Wheelers Cycling Club has had a long association with the town and in
1998 the Tour de France passed through Bray and other areas of County
Wicklow. International Leisure Bowling combines ten-pin bowling,
karting and other leisure facilities. As Bray is a seaside resort, there are many
water sports in the vicinity including Bray Sailing Club, Bray Rowing
Club, Bray Sea Anglers, canoeing, fishing and speedboats.

Bray Heritage Centre and Tourist Office are located in the old
Courthouse, overlooking the bridge. The Tourist Office offers advice on
accommodation and places of interest and stocks a range of books of local
interest. The Heritage Centre explores the historical and geological
heritage of the area. The town has two historical societies – the Old Bray
Society and the Cualann Historical Society – and both offer a series of
lectures and publish their own journals. The new courthouse is located on
Boghall Road.

Within the past decade the town has undergone major improvements.
The Royal Cinema has been extended to a Cineplex. The Main Street has
been upgraded, with new paved footpaths and a traffic-calming system. A
disc parking system operates in the town. The Town Hall, which was built
in 1881, was refurbished in 1993. For a period it housed the Heritage
Centre, a number of restaurants and following a good deal of controversy
it became a McDonald's fast food outlet. Victorian houses on the seafront
and adjoining roads have been modernised and many have been transformed into nursing homes. Modern amusement centres and restaurants
have added to the attractions of the seafront.

SELECT BIBLIOGRAPHY

Annals of the Kingdom of Ireland, The Four Masters, translated by John O'Donovan, Dublin 1860.

Boylan Henry, *A Dictionary of Irish Biography*, Dublin: Gill and Macmillan, 1988.

Bray Journal 1985, Cualann Historical Society, 1985.

Bray Historical Record, Vol. 1 No. 2, Journal of the Old Bray Society, 1986.

Brien, Christopher, *In the Lands of Brien*, Bray, 1984.

Brophy Jim, *By the Banks of the Dargle*, Bray Emmets, 1985.

Bye-laws of Bray Township Commissioners, 1897.

Church of Ireland Registers for Bray Parish.

De Latocnaye, *A Frenchman's Walk Through Ireland, 1796–97*, Belfast: Blackstaff Press.

Doyle, Oliver, and Stephen Hirsch, *Railways in Ireland*, Dublin, 1984.

Flynn, Arthur, *Famous Links with Bray*, Bray: Falcon Press, 1985.

Furlong, Nicky, *Dermot King of Leinster and Foreigners*, Dublin: Anvil, 1973.

Garner, William, Bray: *An Architectural Heritage*, Dublin: An Foras Forbartha, 1980.

100 Years of Bray and Neighbourhood by An Old Inhabitant, Dublin: Carraig Books, 1978.

MacSweeney, James, *The Fight in the Bray Area*.

Moody, T.W. and F.X. Martin, *The Course of Irish History*, Cork: Mercier Press, 1967.

O'Toole, Rev. P.L., *O'Toole's and Other Leinster Septs*, privately published, n.d.

Price, Liam, *The Place Names of County Wicklow*, 7 vols., Dublin: Institute for Advanced Studies, 1957.

Scott, George Digby, *The Stones of Bray*, Bray: Cualann Publications, 1984.

Walsh, Caroline, *The Home of Irish Writers*, Dublin: Anvil Books, 1982.

Directories, periodicals and magazines:

Thom's Directory, Saunder's Newsletter, Wicklow People, The Irish Builder, Bray Parish Magazine, Freeman's Journal, The Dublin Builder, Burke's Peerage, The Irish Times, Dublin Gazette, Bray People, Ireland's Own, Irish Railway Record Society

INDEX